D0537662

Dr. Klaus Bischops/Heinz-Willi Gerards

COACHING TIPS FOR CHILDREN'S SOCCER

Meyer & Meyer Sport

Original title: Tips für Kinderfußball
© 1995 by Meyer & Meyer Verlag, Aachen
Translation: Jean Wanko, Aachen

Die Deutsche Bibliothek – CIP-Einheitsaufnahme

Bischops, Klaus:
Coaching tips for children's soccer / Klaus Bischops ; Heinz-Willy
Gerards. [Transl.: Jean Wanko]. – Aachen : Meyer und Meyer 1999
Dt. Ausg. u.d.T.: Bischops, Klaus: Tips für Kinderfußball
ISBN 3-89124-529-7

© 1999 by Meyer & Meyer Sport, Aachen
Olten (CH), Vienna, Oxford,
Québec, Lansing/ Michigan, Adelaide, Auckland, Johannesburg
Cover design: Walter J. Neumann, N&N Design-Studio, Aachen
Cover exposure: frw, Reiner Wahlen, Aachen
Cover photo: Bongarts Sportfotografie GmbH, Hamburg
Photos: Michael von Fisenne, Aachen
Horstmüller GmbH, Düsseldorf
Figures: Roswitha Hoffmann, Aachen
Printed and bound in Germany by
Burg Verlag & Druck, Gastinger GmbH und Co.KG, Stolberg
e-mail: verlag@meyer-meyer-sports.com
http://www.meyer-meyer-sports.com
ISBN 3-89124-529-7

INTRODUCTION

Soccer as a sport is high on the agenda of our youngest children. Especially children between the ages of six and ten pour into the clubs and play soccer with enthusiasm. There is a continuous interest for children in club sport. One can even record a growth rate.

The large number of young and very young club members naturally puts corresponding demands on the supervisors and trainers of both boys and girls. One is constantly looking for work manuals and incentives, which are a valuable aid in offering training of an appropriately high quality.

This volume devotes itself to children's soccer. "Coaching tips for children's soccer" contains practical suggestions for trainers and club members, who look after young soccer players up to the age of ten. Guiding principles for co-ordinating all the training work are just as important as suggestions for leading a team, for working with the parents or structuring leisure time away from the sports field.

This book is not only successful in its contents, but also, in proven fashion, clearly laid out – all in all a useful teaching manual for day-to-day club work.

Egidius Braun

President
of the German Soccer Association

Seven Speechless Children
Don't Understand the World Anymore

The final whistle! The little mini-soccer players happily wave their arms in the air. They've won. Completely exhausted they creep back into the changing rooms; but their trainer is cross. At the centre of his attack is Michael, just seven years of age: "You move along like a snail. One more such performance and you'll land on the reserve bench." The coach slams the door behind him leaving "his players" sitting there. Seven speechless children don't understand the world any more. They've defeated their opponent but the trainer is cross.

"Unfortunately", according to Klaus Degenhardt, a member of the Soccer Association of the Young People's League for the Middle Rhine area, "this trend can be detected in many kinds of sport. Success is the supervisors' first priority. And they aim to achieve that with all means available." The well-being of the team on the other hand takes second place. Especially where looking after the youngest is concerned, there is a gross lack of appropriate training, which is then replaced by false ambition. Many trainers, supervisors and parents seek to regain through their little ones the success, which they themselves never had in their youth. Children are not mini-professionals. They're looking for fun and a sense of adventure through playing soccer. This must be the guiding principle of training and matches. If one aligns training with the terms of earlier street soccer this strikes a chord with children. So children's soccer needs a framework and rules appropriate to their age-group, at the centre of which is always the relationship with the plaything "ball". In our book "Coaching tips for children's soccer" we would like to help trainers, children, supervisors and youth leaders to organize their work in a child-friendly manner. And so, for that purpose, there are 40 playfully orientated training units for use on the sports ground and 20 for the sports hall. They have been compiled ready for immediate use and can be supplemented with additional games and exercises. However, a children's trainer should also be familiar with some basic principles of child development, so that he can, together with the parents, walk along paths which ensure teaching success. Should children feel at home in a club and in their soccer team, is there any need for further structuring of their leisure time in non-sporting circles?

We, the authors, wish all users of our book great happiness and success in children's soccer.

Klaus Bischops, Heinz-Willi Gerards

Everybody kicks. Not only big and little people, no, even our tiniest tots do it. Everybody kicks a twig or pine cone in the woods, a stone or tin can in the street, a ball in the garden or living room. It's in everyone's nature, and even prohibition orders can't stop people kicking. Whoever walks past a ball quietly lying there without kicking it, has missed out on something in life. Everybody needs to be gripped with the fascination of this round bit of leather.

Clubs know that and are therefore building up more and more teams, especially in the younger age-groups between three and ten years of age. Boys and girls play to excited and enthusiastic mothers and fathers, to coaches, who are just as excited and tearing their hair, because their little protégées don't keep to the agreed tactics. These youngest soccer players play in the original meaning of the word, purely and simply because they enjoy it.

The clubs need to take account of this pleasing development. They need co-workers, who will throw themselves heart and soul into the task of raising the little "star of tomorrow." They must sieze the inbuilt urge to play, develop it further, embellish it and turn it into a junior player, who can mature later into a complete soccer player through carefully calculated training.

A coach often starts with nothing. Only because his son or daughter has the natural urge to play, does he become a coach, without really wanting to. He can hardly expect any assistance, personal experience is of no use at this level and there are very few books on the market.

So it's a pleasure that by means of this book, together with a short section on the development process of this age-group, the task areas of a coach are clearly defined and practical tips given for training and leisure time, beginning with types of play, touching on model lessons right through to leisure-planning and co-operation with parents and club members.

Whoever wishes to immerse themselves in this difficult but attractive work with our "Bambini", should own and use this book.

Klaus Degenhardt
Youth umpire for the Aachen (Germany) district
and member of the Soccer Association of Young People's League
for the Middle Rhine area

10 Theses for Training Children

Training children

▶ should be fun and enjoyable for the children.

▶ must be adapted to the development of the individual.

▶ demands variety in the types of movement offered.

▶ requires an extensive sporting basis.

▶ should bring about a wealth experience in playful form.

▶ must guarantee the child space for experimentation and trying things out.

▶ must adapt to stress put on the level of development and the child's desire to achieve.

▶ incorporates a teaching mandate of encouraging long-term enjoyment of sport and community spirit.

▶ comes to life for children through a personal relationship with the trainer and leader.

▶ should create a positive lifelong attitude to sport.

1. THE STARTING POINT FOR CHILDREN'S SOCCER

In the post-war years children between the ages of ten and twelve found their way into soccer clubs, although they had previously been scuffling about playing soccer in the street. So, on entering a club, they brought with them a certain amount of technical and playful competence, which they'd learnt with each other in the street.

This kind of recreation ground "street" is just not available for today's children. Also there are hardly any other places for children to play soccer with each other, and the structure of family life has changed significantly. Statistics tell us that about 25% of all households with children only have one child in them, 25% of our children live in one-parent-families and 10 - 25% of all children are the victims of divorce. For this reason, many of today's children run the risk of social isolation and must make a concerted effort to find a playmate. No less than 85% of our children are indeed involved in some sort of game and sport, but without any parental supervision. The last statement brings to light a specific desire of children: they are looking for independence, a learning goal, which is often in sharp contrast to parental values and academic demands, but also to the realities of club life. This state of affairs demands a rethink by those responsible for running clubs, but above all by coaches, trainers and co-workers in the field of children's work.

1.1 Children Want to Play

Our children join clubs today at the age of 5 or 6. When they join, time and again they lack incentives to play suitable for their age, because they couldn't acquire any playful grounding in basic skills anywhere. Yes indeed, many children are already limited in their agility, because, so far, they have lacked the space and scope to move about.

Although happy to join a club, at the same time they are cautious. They are happy at the thought of playing, moving about and making new friends, but cautious because of the new and unknown situation they are confronted with. And so it is crucial how a new child is guided into the team by his coach or trainer. Undoubtedly, children have their sporting idols, but no child joins a club with the specific aim of becoming a national player. Thus training children cannot aim to produce national league players or first division players. On the one hand, playing soccer gives the children movement, on the other hand, feelings of happiness, enjoyment, disappointment, anger and rage. A child realises he is an active participant in a game and really lives through the tension and drama of the action. For a child, play is an experience, in which he becomes fully involved and absorbed. He has an inbuilt hatred of monotonous exercises, senseless circuit training and other such adult training procedures, which are foreign to him.

If we are to aim for a 6-year-old still enjoying active soccer when he is 40, we must do everything we can to see that children are fascinated by "Soccer", that it gives them a sense of joy and adventure, and also fires their motivational interest. In the free formation of a soccer game children want to glean their own experience, improve their skill in the game and thus acquire for themselves as many positive situations, i.e. feelings of success as possible.

1.2   A Children's Trainer – Jack of All Trades

If one is aiming for independence above all else in education, then this has its consequences in a trainer's work amongst children. Anyone in a club working with children must surely know that his behaviour and actions must necessarily be of an exemplary nature. Sometimes the trainer becomes a substitute parent, a responsibility which he can find burdensome; and so it is important that he can react, sensitively to the wishes and needs of the children. For example, if it's necessary to correct anyone, then this should be done with obvious sensitivity.

In addition to his human qualifications, a trainer needs to be recognized as a specialist with regard to soccer. We all know that learning amongst this age-group comes from demonstration and imitation. It is precisely the trainer's specialised qualifications which fire the children's enthusiasm and allow him to be their role-model in other areas as well. Each child should be a special individual for him, deserving of his undivided attention and care. Therefore any weakness in the childs' achievement needs helpful encouragement, but also the high-flyers must be brought back to ground level.

This short summary shows that children's trainers must be specially qualified people both in the field of human relations and their subject. Their behaviour determines to what extent children feel at home in their club. It is precisely this "feeling at home in the club" which becomes increasingly important as the child's own family can't always give it the right amount of security and attention which it needs.

Of course, it's possible for older teenagers, senior players who no longer play regularly and fathers and mothers to lead children's training schemes, but they do need thorough pedagogic and specialized training. One does not always find a successful children's trainer in sporting circles. Playing with and training children sometimes yields interesting and unexpected experiences and encounters on a human level.

Thus children find it hard to understand, if one criticizes their efforts. They assume that they have given their very best and have fought to their utmost, even if it all looks very different to the outside observer. Therefore any sort of criticism of their achievements is a depressing experience for younger children, which can rob them of their enjoyment. Positive criticism, praise and recognition of their achievements encourage them and strengthen their determination to succeed. A child-orientated trainer should be able to extract something positive out of a sporting defeat. And so expressions like "You're a disgrace, You're a failure, You're a loser" are totally inappropriate; they only serve to underline the misguided ambition of a trainer and go a long way to undermining the children's feelings.

1.3   Children and Soccer Technique

Children want to play. During a game they test and try out new types of play. It isn't any use trying to train a child's technique by the monotonous practising of detached schemes of movement. They can glean their own experience with a minimal amount of technique; for example, they should be able to receive and deliver a ball to another player as well as shoot goals. With these three prerequisites, children have an adequate foundation for playing soccer. But one can only talk about the child having wealth of experience, if the game takes place in situations which he understands and he gets plenty of contact with the ball at the same time. That is why we play in small groups or teams, for example 3-a-side or 4-a-side.

1.4   The Club and its Soccer Children

A club can, of course, also do a lot for its soccer children outside official training times; but it's precisely such facilities that not nearly enough use is made of.

I.e. that the club

- makes its sports facilities available to all children for them to play in the afternoons.
- sees it that at least one school playground per area of town be free for children to play soccer in the afternoons. The children should play with tennis balls so that no damage is caused.
- provides a playground suitable for soccer for the children in its own area of town.
- seeks a school's co-operation where joint activities can take place.
- offers joint play afternoons or open contests (one street against another, one class against another, etc.)
- opens its sportsground in the holidays for all children, who are keen to play.

1.5   A Closing Word

The soccer ground remains an ideal place to make social contacts, in addition to which it ensures that the activity "Playing soccer" is enthusiastically enjoyed, and at the same time the sort of exercise, which many children lack. One prerequisite is, however, that the club recognizes that there is a need for professional and interactive competence in those responsible for the children. When compared with other activities in which a child is involved, playing on a soccer ground still affords unique experience.

2.   CHILDREN'S SOCCER TODAY

In summing up, we would like to draw attention to the keywords, worthy of note as factors in children's soccer, which have social limitations.

Other leisure possibilities

A

Children today have at their disposal such a wide variety of leisure pursuits including many non-sporting activities, so that everyone can choose what ideally suits them best.

The disappearance of street soccer

B

Children hardly have the space or opportunity to play unhindered, which, in its turn, causes a much more passive structuring of leisure time e.g. with television and videos.

The wrong sort of training

C

In many places children's soccer training has to fit in with that of adults, and it is just this sort of monotonous organisation unsuitable for children which motivates them little, restricts their desire to achieve and fosters disinterest.

Lack of qualified trainer and coaches

D

On the voluntary scene there is a gross lack of qualified trainers and coaches for children's soccer. This area of sports is regulary looked after by casual trainers".

A one-sided attitude to success

E

A misguided striving for success on the part of the children's trainer creates short-term success at the very best, but brings about the long-term collapse of a team. In this sort of system the weaker achievers amongst the children are weeded out and thus lose all their motivation.

3. CHILDREN'S SOCCER DOES HAVE A FUTURE

A

Extension of leisure opportunities

Children's soccer in a sporting context does not just consist of training and competitions. There is a need for new elements to be worked out which inspire the children e.g. smaller competitions, class games etc.; and, in addition to these, the clubs need to extend what they offer to children with innumerable activities of a non-sporting kind. We will go into this in further detail at the end of our book.

B

Revival of the idea "Street soccer"

It goes without saying that most streets today can no longer be used for playing soccer. Therefore clubs should see to it that their own areas of town have "play facilities" permanently available to children. Children must actually like soccer before the training and practising can begin.

C

Training which is adapted to one's age-group

The club is responsible for stimulating a child's enjoyment of the game, whilst at the same time allowing the child's natural urge to play room for creativity and individual development. Also as far as content is concerned, the kind of sporting play an offer must fit in with the child's level of development.

D

Success criteria appropriate to the child

Each child completes its own unique performance development, which can be supported by praise and recognition. Any negative remarks made during or after the game can cause his level of interest in soccer to deteriorate. Even in competitions one should work out how best to primarily serve the interests of the child.

E

How best to win co-workers

The children's trainer should be a known member of the club. He should be able to receive teaching and specialized training, to prove to him that he, his work and his children's teams are being taken seriously. If parents and teachers share the children's enjoyment of soccer, then this should inspire them to share the work-load. But if too much pressure to achieve is apparent, then human irritations occur, which can put off co-workers.

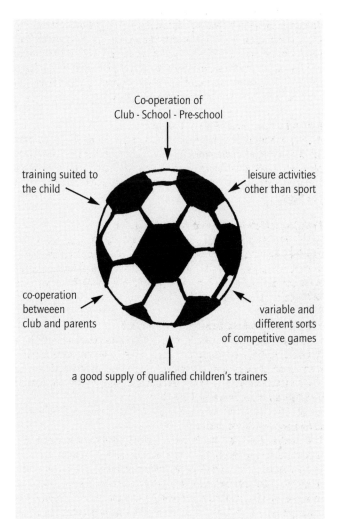

Co-operation of
Club - School - Pre-school

training suited to
the child

leisure activities
other than sport

co-operation
betweeen
club and parents

variable and
different sorts
of competitive games

a good supply of qualified children's trainers

4. WHAT DO CHILDREN LOOK FOR IN A SOCCER CLUB?

Children want to play, play and play again, soccer of course , but also other games like basket ball, indoor hockey, "voelkerball" and many others. They are looking for fun and enjoyment as they play and in their contact with the ball.

A

Children both wish to and must move about. In unrestricted movement exercises they are looking for experience with movement and at the same time, they are improving their general health, mobility and co-ordination.

B

At this age, children demonstrate a great need for new things and thus require a range of games and sports with plenty of variety. Moreover, they should be granted a lot of space for experimenting and trying things out.

C

Children seek social contacts and want to make friendships. They want to play together with others, a need which is not always fulfilled at home.

D

Children live within personal relationships, and so the children's trainer or coach is an important partner in their emotional development.

E

Children look for competition, through which they experience innumerable patterns of behaviour, which can prove to be a valuable experience in real life as well. In a way suited to their own age-group, they want to compare themselves with others and prove their ability in competitive activities, which should however be made interesting and full of variety.

F

Children also seek leisure activities other than sport; and so excursions, hikes, adventure days, holiday camps and much more besides should be offered these days by good sports clubs.

G

What Do Children Want?

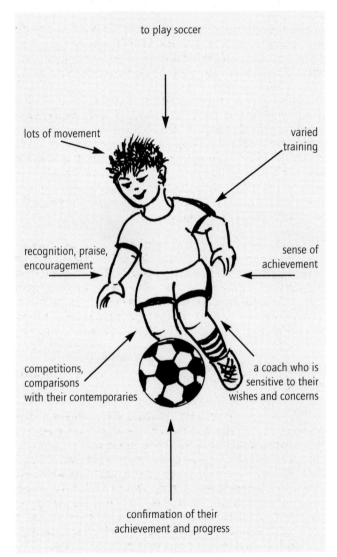

to play soccer

lots of movement

varied training

recognition, praise, encouragement

sense of achievement

competitions, comparisons with their contemporaries

a coach who is sensitive to their wishes and concerns

confirmation of their achievement and progress

5. FROM THE REALM OF DEVELOPMENTAL PSYCHOLOGY

In order to be able to train in a way that suits children also to fulfil the high levels of expectation which link the children to their training in the soccer club, the children's trainer should note the most important stages of development and be able to transfer them to their training.

The primary aim in training children between 5 and 10 is to guarantee the little soccer players a basic and varied programme of movement. To this belongs not only soccer training but also all the many other sporting disciplines such as swimming, track and fields, games, gymnastics using apparatus, etc. This ultimate goal should also be made clear to the parents, so that they understand that soccer training deals with a wide range of sports; it is also true of soccer that only when one's body is trained to peak condition can one get the maximum enjoyment in moving about.

"The extent of the training, the level of difficulty of the individual training exercises and the structure of children's training must be adapted to the individual characteristics of the level of development determined by the age of each child. Therefore it is vitally important that careful attention is paid to the development characteristics of each age-group before setting up a programme of training suitable for and promising success to children and young people." (BRÜGGEMANN 1989)

We include as follows, concisely and clearly, the most important features:

If, during the training of children (5-10-year-olds), we insert another division (up to the age of 6 and 7-10-year-olds) into the realm of developmental psychology, it is because we first want to make clear that the training of a 6-year-old needs a completely different structure than that of a 10-year-old. Secondly, we mustn't overlook interim stages, because development is taking place all the time. Thus a well-developed 7 or 8-year-old, for example, is quite capable of participating in the training of a 10-year-old. It is up to an experienced children's trainer to sensitively adapt the individual amounts of training to the level of development and not its calendar age.

Pre-school/1st year at school (5-6/7 years old)

▷ Coming through of the first permanent tooth.

▷ Ability to co-ordinate i.e. there is a stronger ability to steer apparent from the age of 6, so that combinations like running, catching, throwing, shooting can be learnt slowly.

▷ An all-round, optimistic, basic attitude grows together with the uncritical recognition of the authority of parents and trainer.

▷ A desire to move, play and seek adventure are characteristics of this age-group. A joy in learning and the urge to seek and investigate new things are just some of the aspects which can be used in training.

▷ A desire to play and enjoyment of moving drive the children again and again toward the ball, with the result that they cluster round the ball like a bunch of grapes. A sensible use of the whole field is only achieved gradually and takes a long time.

▷ Children at this age initially only grasp the one basic idea of playing soccer and that is: shooting and preventing goals!

▷ Sense of balance reaches a high level.

Consequences for the trainer

▷ When training this age-group, one doesn't need to make any allowances for differences between the sexes.

▷ Ball sensitivity develops slowly, there are still slight difficulties in timing (calculating the flight of the ball), and children adapt slowly at first to a rolling and jumping ball.

▷ The general motor skills are encouraged by a wide variety of running, catching and relay games incorporating climbing, jumping, gymnastics, rolling and running.

▷ The basic techniques of soccer in its broadest form are practised slowly by continually using the ball.

▷ No particular tests of strength are being trained, but rather by improving co-ordination, a more sensible use of available strength.

▷ Longer achievements of endurance (10-15 minutes) can easily be mastered in a playful way.

Junior school children (7-10 years old)

▷ The first change in physique, increased body length, firstly bringing with it disharmony between bottom and limb measurements.

▷ Because of the increased length, short-term motor liability occurs.

▷ With a gradual improvement in the ability to co-ordinate, the prerequisites for skill in manipulating the ball are improved!

▷ Good prerequisites for basic motor movements are now given in increased measure. "90-95% of the part of the brain responsible for steering movement is already formed." ("fußballtraining" 11/90, p. 4)

▷ "It is rarely possible to improve the output of strength in children up to the age of 10 by specific strength training; this can only be achieved by improved co-ordination of the available muscle potential, because at this age it is rarely possible to cause a transverse increase in size of the muscles." (LIESSEN/HOLLMANN 1977)

▷ The ability and potential to combine skills improve.

Consequences for the trainer

▷ Also at this age specific sex differences are generally insignificant.

▷ At this age, it is possible to detect a rapid increase in motor learning ability, so that technique can now be trained effectively and with marked success. At the same time, the training offered must be playful and graded to suit the children.

▷ Also at this point, there should be no training of strength in the full meaning of the word, but rather a concentration on co-ordination training.

▷ Something which can clearly be improved - between the 7th and 9th year of age is speed. Sprinting ability is clearly way ahead here (Improvement of frequency of movement).

▷ There is an increase in the aerobic endurance performance which can be easily trained, but always in child-friendly forms of play.

▷ Skill and expertise improve at a great rate and allow development by various forms of play, competitive pair-games and obstacle gymnastics.

▷ Combination skill e.g. being able to perform two sporting activities at same time, is now mastered more quickly (e.g. the combination of running and throwing)

▷ Slowly the children can be guided into behavioural patterns determined by their position on field.

▷ Basic techniques (receiving the ball, sending the ball, shooting) are usually learnt by watching and copying. Also no long explanations are necessary, the children just observe what the trainer demonstrates.

▷ Interesting and varied games and ones which don't last too long increase motivation and foster enjoyment in the game.

▷ Technical mistakes are not criticized. The child is shown the matter again and the incident is then connected to further work with a note of praise.

▷ The trainer should constantly be aware of his function as a role model. This applies to his demonstrating exercises, to everything he says and to his behaviour.

▷ Fundamentally the children play in all positions within the team, including goalkeeper. There is no premature specialisation for the 6-9-year-olds and the 8-10-year-olds.

6. TRAINER, COACH, HUMAN BEING, SUPERVISOR ...

Yes indeed, a children's soccer coach must be able to play many roles. He must pick up and encourage, urge on and motivate, comfort and heal, praise and affirm. His heart belongs totally "to his children". Sometimes he must also find the right words of criticism, e.g. when a little "star" forgets, that playing soccer is a team game. Nobody, however strong an achiever they may be, can be permitted to take it into his head to control the whole proceedings alone. Even those players who are lazy in training sessions, stretch the teaching abilities of the trainer just as much as over-ambitious players, who, like children, behave in a much too achievement-orientated way. In such cases, one must intervene at the right time to avoid premature conflicts.

Each soccer player must learn in his early days, to place his achievements at the disposal of the team. A player who only concentrates on his own dribbling and doesn't pass the ball will soon discover, that his team players won't pass to him. The children will thus soon notice, less through words than by accumulated experience of playing, that a team game thrives on the teamwork of the whole team.

A subject not always easy to master is how to get round particularly talented players. They tend to often think that training is only a "necessary evil" for them. The trainer can very quickly eradicate the impression of "throwing one's weight around" by setting up not particularly easy additional exercises for certain players. This course of action ensures considerably greater success from a teaching point of view than many well-meaning words and sees to it that there is no frustrated "talent".

These problems don't only surface during structured training but also in a competitive game. Before the game commences, the trainer should explain to the children how he has put the team together including reserves and explain his choice.

He may also make clear, who comes onto the field at half-time. In doing so he should quietly count on the insight of his players, so that they learn to judge their own ability correctly.

6.1   The Children's Trainer as a Specialist

One ought to be reminded above all of a gradual building-up of the exercise and training sessions, as they are subject to other criteria than those of adults.

Plan for structuring a training unit in children's soccer

A

Introduction

During warming up we get the children into the right mood in a playful way.

Duration: 10-20 minutes

Exercises for getting used to the ball for improving feeling for the ball, playing alone with the ball, room for experimentation, catching, running and relay games, games and exercises for improving co-ordination and mobility training, a versatile psycho-motoric basic training. The trainer gives suggestions, hints and demonstrations.

B

Working it all out

The work-out of new game experiences follows in a playful way.

Duration: 20-30 minutes

Introduction to the basic concepts of soccer: aiming for goals and preventing goals, playing in easily-managed small groups, playful working out of basic techniques by goal-shooting games, goal-keeper training with everyone, games with more or less players than normal, dribbling and passing games. The trainer demonstrates and the players copy him.

C

Competitive games

Even towards the end of a training session, the idea of play is uppermost, moreover completed by the thought of a match.

Duration: 20-30 minutes

Closing games in small groups aiming at goals or baskets, playful ideas culled from other sports, various types of contest.

Keywords for the training programme

▷   The trainer uses the children's natural desire to move about and the childish enjoyment of all play; he sees to it that all the children are constantly moving about.

▷ The ball is always central to the training.

▷ Children seek and need experience of success.

▷ Playful ideas using a ball are of a very challenging nature for children.

▷ During training games: we make up small teams, like one-a-side, two-a-side, or two against three. Most of the time we play at goals with a goalkeeper.

▷ Games should always take place on a small pitch, which is suitable for children.

▷ The balls used must be suitable for the achievement level, which the children have reached.

▷ All the basic skills of soccer must be established playfully, one step at a time and in a way which suits the children.

▷ The trainer must become involved in the learning process of each individual child.

▷ Children enjoy learning, because they seek success, which naturally requires recognition again and again on the part of the trainer.

▷ Every player has a go at all positions, even goalkeeper.

▷ The trainer should give instructions in a simple way, easily understood by the children.

6.2 The Children's Trainer as Coach

Each match, that is to say championship game is a special occasion for the children, which means that the trainer is stretched here not only from a teaching point of view, but also in a professional sense. As trainer, of course, he wants to send a good team out onto the field, make every player aware of his responsibility, clarify his competitive role and also justify the need to swap players in and out of the game, so that the children understand what is going on.

In the psychological and teaching sphere he must rejoice together with his players in their success, give space for newly-acquired skills to be tried out and also instill self-confidence through their success. It's up to him to motivate his players afresh, when mistakes creep in amongst them and they are heading for defeat. But success should also be facilitated for the children according to the situation.
We should now like to give the children's trainer a few tips, which can help him to eliminate problems.

▶ **Punctuality and reliability**
The players must learn right from the start, that they need to be at a meeting point at the agreed time. If they can't manage that, then the trainer/supervisor should be informed promptly i.e. don't wait until 5 minutes before the deadline. In such an instance, it's a good idea to circulate an appropriate telephone number, so that someone can be informed.

▶ **Clean sports equipment**
It should really go without saying, that each player turns up with clean shoes and appropriate sportswear. In the winter or during very bad weather, everyone should have a track-suit with them. The players must be aware from the outset that their outfit says something about the club itself.

▶ **Food before the game**
The question as to what children eat and drink before a game is especially important. The children should understand that large amounts of food and drink before a game have a negative effect, and crisps and Coca-Cola are certainly not to be recommended.

These teaching goals prepared over a long period of time are very important in establishing the children's basic attitude to sport. Therefore they should be discussed with the parents and must be supported by them without fail.

Direct preparation for the game
Even the direct preparation for the game or talking about a game has predominantly teaching characteristics at this age. The trainer should make the following points quite clear:

▶ Although the team wants to win, it doesn't have to do so. That is why it's not the outcome of the game which is in the forefront but rather enjoyment of the game itself.

▶ Thus the trainer should praise his players for good forward kicks, good delivery etc.

▶ The players in the other team are not opponents but partners, and so it's only fair not to block their hard-earned efforts by a foul.

▶ Being replaced by another player hurts a child; but there are other children on the reserve bench, who want to play as well.

▶ If another player makes a mistake, - and lots occur in every game - there is no great fuss. Through their own individual efforts, all other players try and make up for this mistake.

▶ Of course, when putting a team together, overall ability must be considered. So the trainer must explain to the whole team, why he has chosen this particular team arrangement and why any particular position is covered by such and such a player. The little soccer players usually know each other well enough to know who's a good player and who has trained hard.

▶ When giving out the positions the trainer will initially be faced with not insignificant problems, because they will all run after the ball to begin with. Therefore, one begins with rough positioning like attack, mid-field player, defence, goal keeper, left side, right side etc.

▶ Obviously the trainer encounters a few difficulties when drawing up a team. Some of these points have already been addressed in another chapter. At this stage though some desirable intervention from the parents comes into play for the first time. So we are faced with the question, whether the son, whose father always arranges transport for the team, should play again today or not, because he's just not good enough? Should another boy be chosen because his parents sponsor the team regularly? Must a good player necessarily play, when he often plays very selfishly?

Just before the game

About 10-15 minutes before the game starts, the children get themselves into the right mood for playing and warm up a bit. It is here that the trainer can well draw example from the professionals and show that this is what they do prior to each game. But warming up at this age looks rather different. Each child or group of two or three children receives a ball and occupies themselves with it. This can be expanded upon with throwing games in a pre-defined area (circle in the middle, 16 meter area), finishing off with a few attempted goals and small 3-a-side games.

Just before the game, all the players come together, including the reserves, and get themselves into the mood for game. The trainer can give an encouraging word at this point and the team can have a special "shout".

During the game

In addition to his other duties, the trainer should observe the game of his own and the opposing team. Depending on what he observes, it can be necessary to make changes or drop a hint to an individual player. Changing in or out can have been brought about for a variety of reasons. A positive mood can be established during the game depending on what the trainer says. He praises his players, cheers them on and gives them big helping hands. There is no place on the playing field for blame and insulting remarks, especially when one has instilled the idea of fairplay into the players beforehand.

The trainer also has a problem when over-ambitious parents call out during a game, and so a few things should be made clear at the outset. Many parents only see their own child and don't know what has been arranged between the trainer and his team. On the other hand the little players can benefit from fair cheering-on by as many parents as possible.

At half-time

The following patterns of behaviour have proved to be right for the trainer: The players go into the changing rooms or assemble at a corner of the pitch. First of all, the trainer lets the children calm down. Any injuries are dealt with. Each child receives a refreshing drink. After a few minutes of peace and quiet the trainer has his say without any interruption. The trainer expresses his opinion about overall teamwork and then concentrates on individual performance, drawing attention to especially positive features. After that he defines as briefly as possible how play should run in the second half and then sends the children back into play with a word of encouragement. Even at half-time the trainer should speak quietly and sensibly. Any keeping track of mistakes are just as unhelpful as reproach or abuse. If the partnering team proves stronger in terms of achievement, then this should in all fairness be recognized. If the trainer wants to speak to individual players, he should do so with clear instructions.

After the game

If the team has scored a victory, the trainer congratulates all players including the reserves and rejoices with them. If the team suffers defeat, the trainer confirms objectively that the partnering team played better and gives his own players a dose of consolation and encouragement. Because it is always a corporate victory or defeat , there is no need for individual criticism with corresponding pointing the finger in blame. Should any player indulge in criticism of fellow players, the trainer should reject such statements. The trainer ends his little speech with reference to the next training session and what will then be specially practised. On behalf of the club, for whom the children have played, the trainer thanks the whole team for fairplay and wishes them all a safe journey home.

It should be said in conclusion that the coaching of children's teams demands a much wider range of duties from the trainer than, for example, when dealing with seniors. Of prime importance is the realisation that the teaching aspect must always come first.

The Trainer's Duties Surrounding The Game

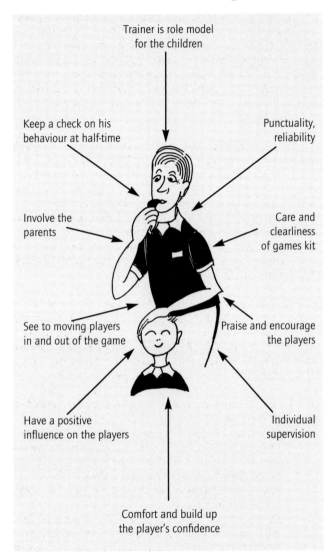

Trainer is role model
for the children

Keep a check on his
behaviour at half-time

Punctuality,
reliability

Involve the
parents

Care and
clearliness
of games kit

See to moving players
in and out of the game

Praise and encourage
the players

Have a positive
influence on the players

Individual
supervision

Comfort and build up
the player's confidence

7.   WORKING TOGETHER WITH THE PARENTS

From all that has been explained so far, it is quite clear that parents have an important role to play in a children's team. On the one hand, the club sees them as helpful co-workers, on the other hand, their presence is not welcome as fanatically one-sided team companions. In summarizing, however, one must realize that no children's team within a soccer club can last indefinitely without parental co-operation and support. This aspect must underly all collaboration between children's trainer and parents.

It is possible to achieve collaboration in various spheres. This partly depends on the willingness of parents and trainer to co-operate with each other and partly depends on the amount of time, the parents can spare for supporting a children's team. Looking at the two factors together, it is really not very encouraging, if parents feel too much is being demanded of them. If this happens, they will very quickly withdraw from their responsibilities. On the other hand, it is not good for working together, if one parent or family tries to take over control of the children's team. So it's important here that the supervisor of the children's team exercises great intuitive care.

Parental involvement should clearly be an express wish of the children's trainer. At the same time of course one is primarily interested in supportive action in certain areas, which the trainer or supervisor can't cover alone. But when parents move into a supportive role, they should be very careful, as it must remain clear to the children, that the trainer has prime responsibility for the team.

Here are are a few ideas as to how parental co-operation can be both helpful and desirable:
- Parents can help get the children to matches by arranging a taxi service, by mutual agreement. This encourages team spirit and takes pressure off club funds. Similar arrangements can be made for journeys to possible training sessions.
- Parents help children to get changed and get their refreshments ready for half-time.
- Parents take over responsibility for washing sports kit. There are various ways of doing this: if all the kit is washed together, which would seem to make most sense as far as the

appearance of the togs is concerned, then this can happen on a changing rota, so that each couple carries the responsibility two or three times each season.

▷ Parents support the trainer by helping him with training. They assume specific functions at the trainer's bidding, so that there are opportunities to differentiate better during training.

▷ Parents standing at the edge of the pitch during an important match don't always behave in a way condoned by the trainer or which sets an example for the children. So here is an issue where the trainer needs to clearly "play" his authority to the parents. Perhaps he can clarify his concept of children's soccer at a parents evening, and appeal to them to support this aim in the interest of their children.

▷ Parents can also step in and help with the preparation of non-sporting activities, which are planned for the children's team.

There is bound to be a wide range of other ideas, with which parents of a children's team or their supervisors can effectively help. With plenty of sensitive co-operation, the children will certainly benefit from the collaboration of their parents and others responsible for their welfare within the club.

It is always a good idea when those responsible for children's teams invite parents to parents meetings. Then any outstanding questions can be answered, problems which have cropped up can be addressed, and general educative guidelines worked out. If these gatherings are given a certain social flavour, then those responsible for the children soon feel drawn into a community, which naturally benefits the club and more importantly the children's teams.

Wherever the parents are granted a look at the decision-making of those responsible for children's and youth work, then their willingness to participate increases. One can see the outworking of this in special situations like when the club decides to run a children's tournament . Then parents can assume responsibility for organisational matters, like looking after invited teams, seeing to the cake and drinks stand, running a lottery, supervising a barbecue and lots more besides.

In conclusion, one should grasp the concept that collaboration of children's supervisors and parents is an essential foundation store for the successful running of a children's team within a club. Therefore, it is well worthwhile to invest a considerable amount of goodwill and ideas.

8.   THE CAPTAIN

Every team engaging in contests or friendly games needs a captain. That also applies to the littlest soccer players. But then we are immediately faced with the question, what should be his specific responsibilities? When dealing with adults and older teenagers, one often refers to the captain as the extended arm of the trainer on the pitch. This function doesn't seem to be quite as important with children's teams although a captain should sense a certain amount of responsibility for the whole team.

However, there is no denying his responsibilities in choosing the referee and welcoming the captain of the partnering team. How best to do this should be work out between the children trainer and his whole team. Perhaps the captain could raise a certain shout when all the team mates are shaking hands together in the changing rooms before the game. Also, should a player out on the pitch insult another player, he can issue a warning to keep quiet.

But how does team acquire a captain? One way of doing it is to let the players vote. Maybe however, the trainer should pick a player, if they don't know each other well enough to choose. Another tactic could be to let a different player be captain at each game, so that all players had a chance to see what was involved, and then decide at the end who was best suited to the task.

If one particular player thus wins the trust of his fellow players through a vote, he automatically becomes a vital link between team and trainer, and so he grows into the role of expressing team wishes to the trainer. Also if he hears that any team member has big problems, he can tell the trainer and get help. If parents behave unfairly during a game, he can have words with them as captain.

To what extent such tasks are applicable to children's teams is the trainer's decision, depending on the current state of his team. But the capacity for assistance should be used to its maximum educative potential in order that the team and all players thrive as well as certain individual responsibility being strengthened.

9. TEAMWORK WITH THE TOP OF THE CLUB

Children's teams are the future of any club, but not just because they are soon to strengthen the club's first team, but because they should learn to enjoy and have fun with sport. The collaboration between the whole youth leadership and presidency of the club are included in this.

Amongst its other responsibilities and duties, the club should ensure that looking after its children's teams has top priority, which in turn means that the club should ensure that its co-workers are properly trained. Moreover, the club should also see to it that the children's trainers receive as much help and support as possible in carrying out their duties. These duties are usually incorporated in the club rules, which should be brought to the notice of the club leaders as and when necessary.

Those responsible for the children's teams should make an effort at all times to be on good terms with the club's leaders, because they need their goodwill and support to fulfill their duties properly. Therefore, club leaders should be invited both to children's team activities, as well as to matches or training sessions. To add a little more weight to an invitation, it should be made into a special occasion. For example the club chairman could speak out some words of encouragement to the children before they play a neighbouring team. Or a member of the club's executive committee could produce something out of his "bag of tricks", because he also used to be a good player.

This bonding to the club grows by means of such signs of liaison between club leadership and children's team. On the other hand, the club directors maintain their position.

10. 40 TRAINING UNITS FOR THE SPORTS GROUND

Soccer is the kind of sport, which is predominantly played out of doors, and so first priority is given to training on the pitch. In this way, children get used to the kind of conditions they will encounter during matches, right from the start. Every sports ground has its own special features, which the players have to adjust to. Of course the ball always follows standard rules, but the constantly changing surroundings test the players afresh each time.

Because the children should learn to control the rolling, flying and jumping ball, the variety of benefits gained from playing on a soccer pitch is much greater than it can possibly be in a sports hall.

For this reason, this place of training is also an excellent preparation ground for the following matches and friendly games. We now present the children's trainers with 40 training units, where the playful character is in the forefront of all units; thoughts of practising and training should be barely detectable. In the first section of each unit, priority is given to improvement of all-round mobility, handling the ball, guiding the ball, rough forms of kicking and the establishment of approximate divisions on the pitch whilst using only a few player's for each game. The second half of each unit does further work at basic technique like receiving the ball, dribbling, types of kicks, improving the players' awareness of space and working on their duelling, behaviour by partner contests. We have divided up the training units on the pitch into three categories:

- Warming-up (15-20 minutes)
- Main emphasis (25-30 minutes)
- Conclusion (25-30 minutes)

In all three areas – and that is what joins them together – the playful element must be central. The idea of contest, constantly joined to the idea of play, is constantly found woven through each unit.

SP 1

Aim: To get used to the ball, experience with the rolling, jumping and flying ball

Warming-up

The challenge is given to start with: "Come on and show what you can do with the ball!" The children get busy with the ball, each for himself. A bit later on, two players come together of their own free will and play with the ball.

Main emphasis

We start with relay games, first without and then with the ball. Each relay team has only 4 players, so that maximum movement is ensured. We're concerned with relay running there and back.

- We run without the ball.
- We carry the ball.
- We toss the ball.
- We guide the ball with our feet.
- We dribble the ball through a little alley of flags.
- The ball is kicked towards the group. The player runs after it and dribbles it back.

Conclusion

To finish off with, we play soccer in our original teams of 4 shooting at goals with goalkeepers. After 5 minutes the partner team is changed over from time to time, until everyone has played against each other.

SP 2

Aim: To get used to the ball and improvement of all-round movement

Warming-up
Each player gets busy with the ball by himself.
▷   We dribble the ball.
▷   When told to we stop the ball and then dribble further.
▷   We dribble in a circle or figure of 8.
▷   We dribble alternately with the right or left foot.

Main emphasis
▷   The ball is held at hip level with both hands, dropped and kicked away.
▷   As above, but now letting the ball tap of and onto the ground and shooting it away.
▷   The ball is held about 1 meter of the ground and then played higher with the thigh.
▷   The ball is thrown into the air and caught above one's head.
▷   The ball is thrown into the air, headed off the forehead and then caught.
▷   Who can demonstrate something special, which the others try to copy?

Conclusion
We set up teams of 3, play into a goal with goalkeeper. After about 5 minutes the teams swap over.

SP 3

Aim: Improvement in all-round co-ordination and getting used to the ball

Warming-up

To begin with, moving around on one's own with the ball.

▶ Cones are set up on a pitch 20 metres square. We dribble the ball round the towers.

▶ At each cone we have run past, we throw the ball into the air and take it on further.

▶ We throw the ball up at each cone, head off the ball and take it on further.

▶ At each cone the ball is stopped and then dribbled further.

Main emphasis

▶ A player stands in goal, 4 players try to kick the ball into goal whilst it is still. Each player has a turn as goalkeeper.

▶ Shooting goals is practised alternately with the left and right foot.

▶ Each player swaps positions with the goalkeeper, once he has scored a goal.

▶ We dribble the ball a few metres towards the goal first and then kick, but with the ball rolling.

▶ We dribble towards the goal and try to dribble past the goalkeeper.

Conclusion

We play 2-a-side towards a little box as goal.

SP 4

Aim: To get used to the ball and improve mobility

Warming-up

Each player is busy with the ball.

> Firstly we dribble with our stronger and then our weaker foot.

> We dribble, stop the ball and dribble further.

> We guide the ball with our foot and run with it down an agreed line.

> Keeping the ball at our feet we constantly change direction.

> Keeping the ball at our feet, we keep on changing speed.

Main emphasis

> The goal mouth is only 1 metre wide. We kick the stationary ball into the goal.

> We dribble towards the goal and shoot from a distance of 8-10 metres at the goal.

> Pairwork. One player stands in goal, the other keeps on shooting goals. They change over, as soon as the goalkeeper has stopped a ball.

> Each player stands in a goal. The goals are about 15 metres apart. Then each player has to both shoot and stop goals, working firstly with shots from 10 metres away, then dribbling, then like a game.

Conclusion

In a 3-a-side match, each plays against the other. Whoever has suffered 2 defeats, is out. The game lasts 7 minutes.

SP 5

Aim: To improve agility and feeling for the ball

Warming-up:
Again we start by moving around on one's own with the ball.

- ▶ The players shoot the ball forward and sprint after it, until they have caught up with it.
- ▶ The ball is thrown into the air and caught above one's head
- ▶ The ball is thrown into the air and as it comes down taken on with the foot.
- ▶ The ball is thrown into the air and headed off again from the forehead.
- ▶ The ball is thrown into the air and played off again from the thigh.

Main emphasis

- ▶ All players dribble their ball backwards and forwards across each other on a marked out pitch. There must be no bumping or body contact whilst doing this.
- ▶ The pitch serving as a dribbling area, is constantly reduced in size.
- ▶ There are innumerable cones on a pitch. Each player should dribble his ball past all the cones and finish with a shot into goal. Whose ball reaches goal first?
- ▶ All the players dribble their ball on the marked out pitch. A player without a ball tries to get the ball off one of the other players. The loser begins the next attempt from another player.

Conclusion
We play 4-a-side with a goalkeeper.

SP 6

Aim: To get used to the ball and improve co-ordination

Warming-up

▶ Day and night
2 teams stand, sit or lie approximately 2-3 metres apart opposite each other. The team which the trainer calls runs to the baseline, before being attacked by the other team.

▶ Pendulum relay
The soccer ball is either dribbled, tossed or kicked by the opposing partner.

Main emphasis

Games in groups of two

▶ The ball is passed backwards and forwards whilst standing at various distances apart.

▶ The ball is passed on whilst running. The pass actually takes place, after the ball has been taken on a few metres. A natural follow-on from this later is the direct pass.

▶ One partner completes a throw to a fellow player, who then takes the ball on with his foot and returns it to the thrower. After a while, roles can be reversed.

▶ One partner passes the ball approximately 2-3 metres from his opposite number, who then tries to stop the ball.

Conclusion

We play 3 against 2 plus a goalkeeper. The team of 2 defends for 5 minutes, whilst the team of 3 attacks, after which roles are reversed.

SP 7

Aim: To get used to the ball and develop an understanding of the game

Warming-up

We warm ourselves up with various shuttle relays.

▶   We run to the opposing partner, rebound and then go to the back.

▶   As above, but we toss the ball.

▶   As above, but we dribble the ball.

▶   As above, but we dribble the ball through cones which have been set up.

▶   As above, but before changing over, the ball is played through a goal one metre wide.

Main emphasis:

▶   Six-to-one

Six players stand on the edge of a circle and pass the ball to each other. An individual player tries to touch the ball and if he succeeds, then he charges position with the last thrower.

▶   Two-to-four

On a marked-out area the 4-man team keeps passing the ball to each other. The 2-man team tries to touch the ball. The 4-man team gets one point for each successful pass, the 2-man team five points for each touch.

Conclusion

We play a tournament with 4-man teams. The teams are organized according to the alphabetical sequence of Christian name initials.

SP 8

Aim: To get used to the ball and shoot goals

Warming-up

▷   Catching game
      4 or 5 players try to strike a fellow player within a limited
      space. One struck, that player crouches down, but can be
      released again by another. After about 2 minutes the
      catchers are swapped over.

▷   Playing alone with the ball
      Each player shows the trainer and fellow players what he can
      already do with the ball. The exercises thus demonstrated are
      copied by the others.

Main emphasis

▷   Chase
      The trainer holds various team bands in his hand and moves
      about with them on a marked-out area. The players must try
      and grab hold of a team band, whilst passing a ball along
      with their feet at the same time.

▷   Goal shooting games
      3 goals are set up, each with its goalkeeper. The players shoot
      the stationary ball at the goal, then shoot after dribbling, and
      finally a goal from a forward kick.

Conclusion

The number 1 chooses!
4 goalkeepers each choose 3 additional players. Now a real
tournament can take place, where each team must play the others.

SP 9

Aim: To improve skill and versatility with the ball

Warming-up

▶   The wall of China
   On the pitch the players run from A to B when the trainer tells them to. If they cross the corridor, a guard tries to strike as many children as possible. Those struck become guards. We play the game firstly without the ball, then tossing the ball, then dribbling the ball.

▶   Working alone with the ball
   Dribbling with the ball at one's feet; kicking the ball and running after it; kicking the ball, and overtaking it before it stops; throwing the ball as high as possible into the air and catching it again in one's hands.

Main emphasis

▶   Two groups stand opposite each other with a distance of 10 metres between them and kick the ball to each other through a small goal.

▶   Who can kick the ball from a distance of 30 metres through a metre wide goal?

▶   Who can kick a ball, which is coming towards him straight back through the goal?

▶   Now we don't aim for the goal, but both goal posts (cones or corner flags).

Conclusion

Everyone has a go at being goalkeeper.
We form 4-man teams, where one player must guard the goal. If the team scores a goal, a new player swaps into goal.

SP 10

Aim: To train feeling for the ball, dribbling and goal shooting

Warming-up

▷ All players work alone with the ball.

▷ Tunnel game

All players dribble the ball in unrestricted space; the trainer is the tunnel player. He runs about relaxed and without a ball, stops from time to time and does the splits. The players must now get the ball through the tunnel as fast as possible.

▷ During a tunnel game only 3 or 4 people are tunnel players.

Main emphasis

▷ Tigerball

All players dribble the ball in an open space. A tiger then tries to chase the ball away from a player. If he succeeds, the player without a ball becomes the tiger.

▷ Tigerball can also be played while tossing the ball with one's hands.

▷ Tigerball becomes more interesting if 2 or 3 tigers chase the ball at the same time.

▷ 4-5 goals are set up on the pitch with a goalkeeper in each one. Who can shoot the most goals in 3-5 minutes?

Conclusion

In a 4-a-side game with goalkeeper, all players are given a number between one and four. Each goal is given as many points as the number of the shooter.

SP 11

Aim: Improving co-ordination and ball sensitivity

Warming-up
Who's afraid of the Big Bad Wolf?
When the trainer says, the players try to run from A to B. The Big Bad Wolf stands in the middle and tries to strike players. These in turn become the Bad Wolf.

▷ We play it first purely as a running game.
▷ Then all the players take part tossing a ball as they go.
▷ Finally a ball is dribbled along.

Main emphasis
Goal mania
We create goals with the cones. There is a player blocking the goal in four of them. Now the players have to get through the fifth open goal with their ball, but the "goal blockers" constantly swap goals.
▷ First we toss the ball with our hands.
▷ Now we guide it with our feet.
▷ We dribble the ball only with the right or left foot.
▷ Whoever manages the same goal twice in succession, gets a special point.

Conclusion
▷ 11 metre king: who can convert the most 11 metre shots into goals.
▷ We play a tournament with 5-man-teams according to the k.o.– system (i.e. as soon as one team has lost a game they are out).

SP 12

Aim: Strengthening co-ordination and getting used to the ball

Warming-up

▷ Swapping balls
Everyone has a ball except two or three players and they all dribble around freely. When the trainer says so, they abandon their own ball and go after a new one. The players who don't manage to get a ball, continue trotting without one. After 5 or 10 minutes, who has always managed to get a ball?

▷ Partner exercises improvising with the ball, where one can do as one pleases.

Main emphasis

Practising goal shooting

▷ We dribble towards the goal and finally shoot.

▷ We dribble through a slalom of flags and shoot at the goal.

▷ Firstly dribbling, then alternate kicks with the right or left foot.

▷ Instead of a goalkeeper, there are tyres hanging in the goal. They are marked with various numbers. Whoever shoots a goal through a tyre scores that number of points.

▷ This competition can also be transferred to a team game.

Conclusion

▷ Keep the pitch clear!
Team A kicks the ball onto pitch B and vice versa. Which team has the least number of balls on the pitch when the whistle goes?

▷ Tournament with 3-man teams and goalkeepers in each goal.

SP 13

Aim: To develop one's understanding of the game

Warming-up

▶ Each player is busy with the ball by himself.
▶ We show what we can already do with the ball; tricks, various delusions, fast change of direction etc.
▶ Individual players demonstrate new tricks, which are then copied by the others.
▶ Fast short sprints (10-15 metres) kicking the ball along.

Main emphasis

▶ Driving the ball
Two players stand opposite each other with 20 metres between them. A shoots the ball as far as possible, B tries to intercept the ball (with hand or foot) and can then shoot back from where he has caught it. Who can drive his partner over the base line?
▶ Shot into goal after a pass
The trainer or a supervisor passes the ball and the player then has a shot at the goal.
▶ Passing whilst moving
The ball is passed backwards and forwards between two players whilst they are moving forwards.

Conclusion

▶ We pull our partners across a line.
▶ Who can turn his partner from his tummy onto his back?
▶ We play towards two young people's goals for the first time with 6-man teams diagonally across the pitch.

SP 14

Aim: To improve movement and skill

Warming-up

▶ Playing alone with the ball paying special attention to guiding it in a confined space, change of direction and speed.

▶ Pendulum relay
The first players who are standing opposite each other dribble towards each other. When they meet, they dribble round each other and run back to their group. Then the next runner takes over.

▶ The ball should be shot from the penalty line across the centre line, first from a stationary position, then whilst dribbling, finally from the hand.

Main emphasis

▶ Billiard-Soccer
Two players, each with a ball, play opposite each other and each tries to hit the other one's ball with his ball. Each hit scores a point.

Tricks using the ball

▶ We lift the ball up with our feet.

▶ We trap the ball between our feet and juggle it up our legs.

▶ We juggle the ball, which is allowed to tap on and off the floor in between times.

▶ We toss the ball whilst standing on one leg.

▶ We throw the ball up. Catch it again whilst standing on one leg.

Conclusion

▶ Play one to one into little flag goals.

▶ Play two against two into little flag goals.

▶ After play is over, we run once more up and down all lines on the pitch.

SP 15

Aim: To improve ball sensitivity and playing together

Warming-up

▷ A catching game without the ball. About 50% of the players try to catch the others.

▷ We set up groups of four, which we number. Then the first group catches the second whilst 3 and 4 rest, then the third catches the fourth etc.

▷ Again with numbered groups of four, in which the first catches all the rest, then the second all the rest etc.

▷ The soccer snake
About 5 players run along kicking the ball one behind the other. The first player gives ideas for the others to copy.

Main emphasis:

▷ Hare and hunter
All the players are hares and three players are hunters. The hares move around in the penalty area. The hunters try and shoot at the hares.

▷ Atomic soccer
All players sit in the penalty area next to their ball. A player, "the atom", runs about with his ball shooting it gently at the seated players, who then stand up and begin dribbling their balls likewise. If the "atom" shouts "stop" then all the players must sit down again.

Conclusion

▷ Shooting from positions
5-8 balls lie round the goal mouth ready for shooting. Who can score the most goals?

▷ In a 5-a-side match positions are given out for the first time: goalkeeper, 2 defence, 2 attack

SP 16

Aim: To improve playing together and one's ability to react

Warming-up
▶ Chain catching
  One player strikes another in the penalty area. They then join
  hands and strike other players. As soon as players have made
  a chain, that chain divides into two new ones.
▶ Driving the ball
  The ball is shot as far as possible out of the hand. The partner
  catches it and shoots it back.

Main emphasis
▶ Hunter ball with time limit
  2 teams are drawn up. Team A (hares) stand off the pitch,
  Team B (hunters) on the pitch, each with a ball. Then the first
  hare runs onto the pitch. If he's hit, then the second hare
  follows etc. How long does it take a team to get all the hares?
▶ Of course the hares can also be set up with a ball, which they
  must kick along.
▶ The hunters only have one ball, which they can throw to each
  other.

Conclusion
Two goalkeepers
We play a tournament with 4-man teams, but this time the goal is
twice as big and so there are two goalkeepers in each goal. If one
goalkeeper registers a goal, he is replaced in goal by a field player.

SP 17

Aim: To train versatility and attitude to the game

Warming-up

▷ The moving goal
The trainer/ supervisor runs around slowly holding a gymnastic baton on each side at chest height. The players shoot their balls through underneath the batons and thus score the maximum number of goals.

▷ 5 in a circle and another runs
5 players form a circle and play the ball to each other. One player in the circle tries to get the ball away.

Main emphasis

▷ Two players pass the ball backwards and forwards to each other whilst moving.

▷ The passes should be as far apart as possible.

▷ We play a drop-kick or flying ball to our partner from our hand.

▷ One partner throws the ball up in the air and heads it towards a fellow player.

▷ The ball is thrown to a fellow player and caught.

▷ The ball is thrown to a fellow player, who heads it back.

Conclusion

▷ Two little flag goals stand opposite each other 5 metres apart. Each player throws the ball into the air and heads it into the opposite goal.

▷ The goalkeeper scores points. A tournament is played with 4-man teams including goalkeeper. It's the goals which count. But for each goal, which their own goalkeeper stops, the team gets one bonus point.

SP 18

Aim: Improvement of basic technique

Warming-up

▶ Each player does some intensive ball work, during which a prime aim should be to keep the ball off the ground for a long time

▶ Hitting balls
On a pre-marked pitch, all the players dribble their balls. Everyone wants to hit somebody else's ball. If a ball leaves the marked area, then the player has to dribble his ball once right round the whole marked pitch, before he can play again. Who shoots most balls off the pitch?

Main emphasis

▶ Running for a minute with the ball
Each player dribbles the ball for a minute. If he thinks that time is up, he stops and puts his foot on the ball. So that everyone learns to estimate time properly, this exercise is repeated many times.

▶ Shooting off little hats
We draw up 3-man teams. 5 to 10 little hats stand on the baselines of the pitch. Each team must defend its own little hats and shoot round the other teams little hats.

Conclusion

▶ Catching dogs
Two 5-man teams stand alternately next to each other on the goal line. Team A has chosen a player in advance to be a dog, who suddenly runs off barking loudly and must be caught by the opposing team before he reaches the (6 metre) line.

SP 19

Aim: To improve one's skill with the ball

Warming-up

▷ Car game

All the players move around a prescribed pitch. The trainer says "We'll run in first, second, third or fourth gear." The game is played first without, and then with the ball.

▷ Shadow running

All movements made by the man at the front are to be copied by the others. Firstly as a run in pairs changing directions (at the trainer's bidding), then in groups of five.

Main emphasis

▷ Goal champion

Play is directed towards a goal with goalkeeper. Four children want to shoot goals, but individually. Whoever scores a goal, becomes goalkeeper.

▷ Ball theft

Each player has a ball to dribble with. The trainer tries to steal the ball from the players. If he succeeds, the trainer then shoots the ball a long way away. The player must retrieve his ball and carries on playing.

Conclusion

▷ Swapping numbers

Two 4-man teams play against each other. Each player within the team gets a number. If a player scores a goal, he swaps over with the same numbered player from the other team.

SP 20

Aim: To improve ball control and playing together

Warming-up

▷   Stealing bands
     Each player has stuffed a team-colour band into the back of
     his trousers. The aim is then to steal the bands of the other
     players whilst defending one's own.

▷   Work with the ball
     We guide the ball and then do a forward-roll. We dribble the
     ball and do three press-ups. We shoot the ball into the air, do
     another forward-roll and then catch the ball again. We hold
     the ball up in the air for a long while.

Main emphasis

▷   Goal shots
     We divide into pairs. The trainer plays the ball first, a pair
     sprints after him and struggles to get the ball. The victor
     shoots at the goal. The same contest takes place as above,
     but this time beginning on ones back/ on one's tummy. Both
     partners stand back to back. The trainer decides at the last
     minute, whether he will play the ball forwards or backwards.

Conclusion

Tournaments one-to-one
We form 3-man groups. One player does the splits to form a goal. The
other two play one-to-one. Goals may be shot from both sides.
Whoever has just scored a goal, becomes goalkeeper.

SP 21

Aim: To receive and take the ball on further

Warming-up

▶ The players work in a relaxed way with the ball.

▶ We pick the ball up in our hands, drop it and carry on with both feet.

▶ We throw the ball up, head it off and then carry on with our feet.

▶ We drop the ball out of our hands onto our knees, push it up high and then collect the falling ball with our feet.

Main emphasis

▶ Hitting little hats

On a limited bit of field space there are 5 to 8 little hats. 3-4 players defend the hats and shoot the other players' balls away. All the other players want to hit a little hat with their balls.

▶ Receiving the ball

The trainer plays a ball to a player who is running towards him, and who takes it on whilst still running.

▶ Direct play

The trainer plays a ball to a player, who is running towards him, who then plays it straight back to the trainer.

Conclusion

▶ 2 players play the ball in the direction of the goal, running all the time.

▶ We play 2-a-side towards 2 little goals (1 metre wide) without goalkeeper.

SP 22

Aim: To improve one's attitude towards the game and general versatility

Warming-up

▶ Numbers race

We draw up several teams, which, having been numbered from front to back, stand in a line, sit or lie. When the trainer calls out a number, the relevant players run once round their little flag back to their place. He who gets there first, scores a point.

▶ Trailer relay

Using the same starting position, the players run one at a time round the little flag and back to their places.

Main emphasis:

▶ We play 3 against 1 at a little goal. Goals can be shot from either side.

▶ Then we play 5 against 2, but this time with a goalkeeper in goal.

▶ We play 2 against 1 at a goal with goalkeeper. He who scores a goal becomes the single player.

Conclusion

▶ For the first time we play 7-a-side in half a match at 2 goals with 1 goalkeeper. This time we don't want any dribbling. Whoever happens to have the ball must stand still and pass it. If a player runs more than 5 paces with the ball, the other then gets a free kick.

▶ Shooting goals

We dribble the ball along the outside, but parallel to the goal and shoot from the corner at the goal. We play this from the right and the left.

SP 23

Aim: To improve one's attitude towards the game

Warming-up

▷   We begin by juggling the ball, where the ball may touch the ground.

▷   We balance alternately with the right and left foot.

▷   Handball without any goals
     We draw up two equally-strong teams. Each pass gets a point. Who can score the most points in 5 minutes? The other team tries to take the ball away and score points for themselves.

Main emphasis

▷   In a pre-marked pitch we play four against one. Each player of the 4-man team may only have two and later only one contact with the ball.

▷   Hitting players
     In a pre-marked pitch everyone plays against each other, but only one player can be hit with a headed ball i.e. someone throws a ball into the air and, by heading it, hits a fellow player.

▷   Using the same game again, we have four areas in a row. Everyone starts in the first area. Whoever has "beheaded" a player, moves into the next area. Who reaches the fourth field first?

Conclusion

▷   One-footed soccer
     We draw up 3-man teams and play a tournament aiming for two goals with goalkeeper. In the first round, one can only play with the left foot, in the second with the right foot and in the third round everyone plays with his weaker foot.

SP 24

Aim: To improve basic technique and understanding of the game

Warming-up
▷   We toss the ball in an upright position with both left and right hands and whilst moving.
▷   We toss our ball and try to knock balls away from other players.
▷   We guide the ball with left and right foot alternately, and using the inside and outside of our feet.
▷   Whilst guiding the ball, we try to shoot the ball away from a fellow player.

Main emphasis
We complete one stage after another with a partner.
▷   1st station: At each throw, we pass the ball to each other.
▷   2nd station: We kick the ball to each other off the front of our foot.
▷   3rd station: We play the ball to each other while running and end with a shot into goal.
▷   4th station: We head the thrown ball back to our partner.
▷   5th station: We play 1-a-side at 2 little goals without goalkeeper.

Conclusion:
▷   We play 4 against 3 at 2 little goals without goalkeepers. At the end of the game, the goals are multiplied by the number of players in the other team. Thus the winner is identified.
▷   All players whose names run from A to L, play against the other players M to Z. As all players are involved in the game, three balls are used simultaneously.

SP 25

Aim: To improve one's attitude to the game

Warming-up
▶ We get busy with the ball.
▶ We put the ball in front of us and sprint after it.
▶ We shoot the ball from our hand into the air and then stop it.
▶ We shoot the ball into the air and run on as the ball is coming down.
▶ We keep the ball in the air as long as possible.
▶ We throw the ball over our heads from one hand to the other.
▶ We pull the ball over our heads with our foot, turn round and catch it again.

Main emphasis
▶ A triangular goal is set up in the middle of the field, first without goalkeeper (1 metre wide), then with goalkeeper (4 metres wide). Two 4-man teams play each other and can shoot goals from all sides.
▶ In a 3-a-side game only one player per team may shoot. He is chosen by his team. If he succeeds in shooting a goal, another player takes over the role.

Conclusion
All players are divided between two teams. Each team, which is losing after goals have been scored, can select a player from the other side.

SP 26

Aim: To improve one's technique with the ball

Warming-up

▷ Atoms game
The players run around in a defined space. The trainer calls out a number and the players form groups of that number.

▷ Clearing the penalty area
All balls are on the ground and two players are in the penalty area. The remaining players spread out round the penalty area. Both players shoot all the balls out of the penalty area; the other players shoot them back again.

Main emphasis

▷ Mirror handball
One player tosses the ball up, down, to right and left. The partner does exactly the same but mirroring the actions.

▷ Mirror soccer
One player dribbles to the right, to the left, slowly, fast. The partner mirrors all of those actions.

▷ Swapping partners
One player dribbles the ball along past a fellow player. The partner can only take one step to the side.

Conclusion

Today a tournament has been arranged with 3-man teams without goalkeeper.

A	1:2 / 3:4 / 5:6
B	3:1 / 2:5 / 4:6
C	5:3 / 6:2 / 1:4
D	2:4 / 1:5 / 3:6
E	1:6 / 3:2 / 4:5

SP 27

Aim: To gain playing skill

Warming-up

▷   Pendulum relay with obstacles
The aim is to jump over one obstacle, climb under another, do one forward roll, one backward roll and then shoot a ball into goal.

▷   Competitive moving ball
The teams line up one behind another, pass a ball over their heads or through their legs to the back. The last player dashes to the front.

▷   Pendulum relay with a football
The player runs as far as the middle and then shoots the ball to his opposite number.

Main emphasis

▷   In the middle of the centre circle is a 1-metre-wide goal. Two teams take up their positions on both sides of the centre line. Each team tries to shoot as many goals as possible into goal.

▷   The goal on the middle line is now 4 metres wide and has two goalkeepers. Again, both teams try and shoot goals.

▷   From half right or half left dribble towards the goal and with the front of ones foot attempt a shot at the goal.

Conclusion

▷   The wrong sort of soccer
4-man teams play each other with two different-coloured balls. Goals with balls of one colour score twice as many goals, but goals scored with the other colour are deducted.

SP 28

Aim: To improve ball control and playing together

Warming-up

▷   Catching game in the penalty area
        One catcher tries to hit the other players, whilst a ball is
        being thrown from child to child. Whoever has the ball
        cannot be hit.
▷   The same game as above, but the ball is kicked to each other.
▷   Guiding the ball with stakes
        Guiding the ball with a forward roll, 3 press-ups, putting it
        down and running after it, shooting it into the air and
        stopping it.

Main emphasis

Who's going to be dribbling king?
▷   We dribble in a confined space without bumping anyone.
▷   When the whistle goes, stop the ball and dribble in another
        direction.
▷   We dribble circles to the left and to the right, doing a figure
        of eight or a question mark.
▷   When the whistle goes, pick the ball up, throw it into the air
        and carry on dribbling when it comes down.
▷   The ball is guided with the weaker foot.
▷   We guide the ball with the inside or outside of the foot.

Conclusion

▷   We play 2 against 4. The 4-man team's goal is twice as wide.
▷   We play 5 against 3. The minority team has a goalkeeper,
        although both goals are 3 metres wide.

SP 29

Aim: To improve guiding the ball

Warming-up

 Everyone is busy with the ball, concentrating above all else on practising moving the ball on very quickly.

Shadow dribbling as partner
The second player follows the first and copies his movements.

"Help me, brother"!
One of the players who has been hit by a catcher in a confined space must stand still. He can be "rescued" by calling "Help me, brother". After the shout, a fellow player gives him a hand and thus releases him.

Main emphasis

Out of the box of tricks
Trying to trick another from the right, but passing on the left; stepping over and spurting on with the ball; playing the ball through the legs; etc.

The silly sheep
In each 4-man team a silly sheep is hiding. The trainer quietly gives him a number. If that number or a multiple of it is reached during play, he then plays the ball to the other team. Both teams should guess the number. Who manages it first?

Conclusion

Shooting goals as partners
Two players stand behind one another. The one at the front does the splits, the one behind plays the ball through his legs. Both race after it, struggle for the ball and finish with a shot into goal.

SP 30

Aim: To improve feeling for the game

Warming-up

- Everyone is busy with the ball concentrating on heading and juggling with it.
- Guiding the ball with the left and right foot, with the inside and outside of the foot.
- We run in curves with the ball.
- We run the initials of our forenames.
- We build tricks and deceptions into our running.
- While running full tilt we try and shoot goals.

Main emphasis
Partnerwork with the ball

- We play the ball along the ground to each other.
- We play the ball as a flying ball (i.e. without its touching the ground)
- With each throw, we throw the ball to our partner, who heads it back.
- As balls are thrown, they are stopped at the chest.
- We play double passes on the spot.
- We juggle the ball in the air, during which one takes the ball from someone else. In between times, the ball may touch the floor, but then we carry on playing.

Conclusion

- In a match we play two against two towards two goals each with goalkeeper. Each goal scored after a double pass, counts as two goals.
- In a match with 3-man teams aiming at goals without goalkeeper, the goal scorer alternates his team.

SP 31

Aim: To improve technique and train co-ordination

Warming-up

▶   Keep the box full
     A box is full of balls. A player throws the balls out of the box. The rest of the players fetch the balls back with their feet and put them in the box.

▶   We run a few times round the penalty area. On one of the long sides we do a hopping run, hop with the right and then the left leg, then run with turns and quick spurts.

Main emphasis

▶   Stations-Training in pairs
     Station 1: We juggle the ball
     Station 2: We carry out a slalom-dribble as a kind of chasing race.
     Station 3: We throw the ball to someone and head it back.
     Station 4: We throw the ball to someone and stop it with our feet.
     Station 5: One shoots the goal, the other is goalkeeper.
     Station 6: One shoots the ball up high, the other stops it.

▶   Defending cones
     One player defends a cone, three players shoot at it.

Conclusion

▶   Continuous soccer with a break
     We play a normal tournament with a 4-man team at goals with goalkeepers. Whoever has just scored a goal, has as rest until the next goal is scored.

SP 32

Aim: To improve basic technique

Warming-up

▷ Each player is busy with the ball by himself.

▷ At warming-up speed, we play the ball to each other, dribble it, shoot it ahead and sprint after it. These exercises are interrupted by the trainer's shouts, as he gives instructions: e.g. crouch down, forward roll or backward roll, heading jumps, press-up, turning jumps.

▷ Ball skill

The trainer demonstrates certain movements with the ball which all the players copy.

Main emphasis

▷ Training techniques in stages

Stage 1: We practise throws to our partner.

Stage 2: Both partners stand next to each other. One partner shoots the ball forwards. Both sprint after it.

Stage 3: We head the ball backwards and forwards to each other as often as possible.

Stage 4: We keep on with direct passing of the ball.

Stage 5: How many shots does it take for a player to cover the whole field? The partner takes it back again.

Stage 6: Alternating throwing the ball in the air, heading it, running after and stopping it.

Conclusion

3-man teams now play towards two 1-metre goals placed one behind the other. If the ball goes through both goals, the team gets 2 points.

SP 33

Aim: To improve duelling strength

Warming-up

▷   Relay competitions
We warm ourselves up by relay races there and back with a few exercises thrown in e.g. a heading jump without a ball, a complete turn on one's own axis, four-footed walk, hopping on one leg etc.

▷   In a confined space, we play 5 against 2. Having started in the penalty area, the space gets less and less until the goal circle.

Main emphasis

In the foreground contests between partners are taking place. We trot around in between these for two minutes.

▷   Press-ups contest.

▷   The partners sit back to back, arms interlinked. Then each tries to pull his partner to the left or right.

▷   The partners sit opposite each other legs at an angle. One with his legs inside (his partner's) the other outside. The one, whose legs are inside, pushes his partner's legs outwards, but this is opposed.

▷   Pulling contest.

▷   Cock fight.

Conclusion

We play with 7-a-side teams on half the pitch. One team has to shoot into the big goal, the other team into 2 little goals (1 metre wide) but without goalkeeper, which have been set up on the side lines. Who shoots the most goals?

SP 34

Aim: To improve corporate play

Warming-up

▷   Everyone guides the ball in the centre circle. Each corner flag is given a name. When the trainer calls a name, all the players dribble to this corner flag.

▷   In the same game, the ball is guided with the weaker foot.

▷   Who can shoot his ball from a corner flag, so that it stops in the centre circle?

▷   Catching in tens
      Two teams are drawn up. The team with the ball must now manage 10 passes, without the other team touching the ball.

Main emphasis

▷   We play 2 against 2 into little goals.

▷   We play one-to-one into little goals.

▷   We play 3 against 1, where the individual player may defend with his hand.

▷   We play 3 against 3, alternating between 5 minutes soccer and 5 minutes handball.

▷   We play 3-a-side rugby. The ball may be passed on by hand or by foot.

Conclusion

▷   Little against big
      We make up 2 teams from 6 players. The three littlest players play against the three biggest. Who is more successful, little or big?

SP 35

Aim: To improve speed

Warming-up
Different types of passes in fours
▶ The ball is passed along a row.
▶ The ball is passed anyway you like.
▶ All players are on the move passing the ball.
▶ All players stand next to each other and sprint after the ball once passed.
▶ The ball is kept in the air as long as possible during passes.
▶ The ball is played on further immediately after passing.
▶ The 4 players pass the ball to each other whilst running towards the goal. One person finishes with a shot into goal.

Main emphasis
We train speed
▶ 5 sprints over 10 metres with breaks.
▶ 3 sprints over 10 metres guiding the ball.
▶ 3 shots, sprinting after, and overtaking the ball.
▶ Zigzag sprinting with the ball round little cones.
▶ Slow trotting with the ball at one's feet and then, when the trainers says so, a 10-metre sprint.
▶ In teams of three we play into 2 goals with goalkeepers. The goalkeepers must hit the ball forwards out of their hand again, once its been caught.

Conclusion
We play a tournament with teams of 7, each against the other in 7-minute games.

SP 36

Aim: To improve goal shooting and playing together

Warming-up
Playing alone with the ball
▷ We guide the ball along close to our feet, first the right foot and then the left.
▷ We guide the ball with our feet and vary the speed.
▷ We guide the ball with our feet, constantly changing direction.
▷ We guide the ball with our feet incorporating various tricks, as if we were outplaying a player.
▷ We guide the ball with our feet, shoot it and then sprint after it.

Main emphasis
Goal-shooting training in stages
▷   1. We shoot the ball whilst stationary along the ground towards the goal.
▷   2. We shoot the ball after dribbling it along the ground towards the goal.
▷   3. We shoot the ball whilst stationary along the ground towards the goal with our weak foot.
▷   4. We dribble past one of the defence and shoot at goal.
▷   5. We dribble towards the goal and play the ball past the emerging goalkeeper into goal.
▷   6. We throw the ball into the air and shoot towards goal.

Conclusion
We play against each other with 7-a-side teams including a goalkeeper. In the first round each player may only touch the ball twice. In the second round each ball must be played directly from player to player.

SP 37

Aim: To improve playing together

Warming-up

▶ Triangular runs

Each player guides the ball with his foot completing a triangle. The first side slowly, the second faster, the third sprinting.

▶ This time in the following sequence: 1st side walking, 2nd side putting the ball down and sprinting after it, 3rd side running down to the end.

▶ New sequence: 1st side with the ball at our feet, 2nd side heading the ball from the side of our heads, 3rd side tossing the ball.

▶ Final sequence: 1st side throwing the ball and running after it, 2nd side balancing the ball, 3rd side guiding the ball with our feet.

Main emphasis

▶ Passing through little cone goals

A marked-out playing area has 8-10 little cone goals (1 metre wide). The players only pass the ball to each other through the cone goals. It all takes place in pairs.

▶ Duelling behaviour:

In a one-to-one contest the ball is shielded with the body.

▶ We pass the ball to our partner through our legs and both then sprint after it.

▶ One pair stands next to each other. One shoots the ball in whichever direction he likes and both sprint after it.

Conclusion

We play a tournament with 6-a-side teams. The winning team can say what they would like to do in the next training session.

SP 38

Aim: To improve ball sensitivity

Warming-up

We engage in different types of passing in groups of 3.

▷ Passing the ball with stopping and carrying on playing.
▷ Direct passing of the ball.
▷ Passing the ball with stopping and carrying on playing with the weaker foot.
▷ Direct passing of the ball with the weaker foot.
▷ Keeping the ball in the air whilst passing.
▷ Passing "flying balls" to each other.
▷ Playing long shots to each other from the hand.

Main emphasis

▷ Goal shooting competition
Two teams stand about 25-30 metres from the front of the goal. A slalom course is built up in between. When told to go, both players set out dribbling. Whoever reaches the 11 metre mark first, shoots at goal. The other player dribbles once more round the last flagpole and then shoots at goal.

▷ Goal shooting competition with names
This time the trainer calls a player from each team by name. Then the same sort of contest ensues.

Conclusion

▷ Minority game
We play 5 against 3 with frequent change of the teams.
▷ We run and touch all 4 corner flags.

SP 39

Aim: To improve game technique

Warming up

▶   A chasing race round a marked-out square (each side 10-15 metres long): The whole group is divided into 4 teams, who stand in a corner of the square. When told to go, they sprint off and catch up with a runner from the front team, first without a ball, then with a ball being tossed, then with a ball being kicked.

▶   Traffic police
4 teams run when the trainer says, always diagonally, sometimes without the ball, or tossing the ball or dribbling the ball.

Main emphasis

We train various tricks with the ball.

▶   We trap the ball between our feet, jostle it upwards and catch it again with our hands.

▶   We throw the ball through our legs whilst doing the splits and catch it.

▶   We take the ball behind our backs, throw it over one shoulder and catch it.

▶   We throw the ball up in the air, touch the ground with one hand, then catch the ball again.

▶   We throw the ball up in the air, turn right round once and catch the ball again.

Conclusion

We play with two 3-a-side teams towards a goal without goalkeeper, and tyres are hanging in the goal. A goal is scored when the player has shot the ball through a tyre.

SP 40

Aim: To train mobility and to improve one's attitude to the game

Warming up

Partnergames

▷   We pass the moving ball on the inside and outside of our foot.

▷   Shooting with our hands, we drive the ball across the entire pitch.

▷   With throws-in (from the sideline), we drive the ball across the entire pitch.

▷   One partner throws the ball, the other heads it back.

▷   One partner throws the ball, the other heads it with a header-jump.

▷   The person with the ball protects it with his body, the partner gets the ball from him.

Main emphasis

▷   Number dribbling

On one pitch numbers lie spread out on the ground. All the players dribble round them. Suddenly the trainer calls a number, and everyone dribbles towards that number.

▷   Showing numbers

This time the trainer shows a number which they must dribble towards and so the players must take their eyes off the ball.

▷   Solving problems

Now the trainer sets up a calculation problem e.g. $24:8 = x$ or $7-5 = x$. The players work out the answer and run up to that number.

Conclusion

We draw up 7-a-side teams including goalkeeper and play a tournament to find the club champions.

In principle, the same terms apply to children's training in the gym as outside on the soccer pitch and yet the conditions are a little different.

For example the gym floor is level, making ball movements more predictable, which is bound to be a relief for beginners. On the other hand, the hardness of the gym floor changes the actions and reactions of the ball.

As the children should be aiming to experience handling a rolling, jumping and flying ball, this kind of alternative football pitch is undoubtedly an enriching and profitable experience.

Many games, designed in our book for the soccer pitch, can obviously be adapted for use in a sports hall with minimal variations. Moreover a sports hall contains some additional elements because of its side walls and end walls, which can make a game considerably more interesting.

There now follow 20 training units for use in a sports hall, which can either be used with the children as described or in other combinations. Therefore, we have divided each unit into two main sections, a basic grounding in mobility and attitude towards the game, which is as versatile as possible and also a section which concentrates on soccer.

Hint:
When using the indoor-gym apparatus, the trainer should check for himself in advance that individual pieces of apparatus are properly set up and make everything safe by using mats.

H 1

Aim: To gain mobility experience and to get used to the ball

Main points

All-round basic training

▶ Keep the box full

Part of a box is filled with lots of balls. The trainer or a player throws the balls as fast as possible out of the box. All the players collect them up and put them back in the box.

▶ Empty 2 boxes

2 boxes 5 metres apart are full of balls. One player throws the balls out again. The other players play the balls, guiding them with their feet, back to one of the boxes.

▶ Hand on the line

During a pendulum relay, the ball is led along with the foot. If a player crosses a line, he must touch it with his hand on the ground.

Playful soccer training

▶ Sitting soccer

All the children are divided into 2 teams. Soccer is now played in a crab-like walk, and goal is a mattress leant up against the front wall.

▶ Shooting goals

Several mat goals without goalkeeper are set up against the wall, and then each player can shoot 5 times at the goal. Then he runs to the next mat goal. Who gets as many goals as possible?

▶ Closing game

In each half of the sports hall we play a small tournament with 3 players in each team.

H 2

Aim: To improve various types of movement and getting used to the ball

Main points
All-round basic training

▷ Running on the line
We run at various speed on the lines round the hall: red line = slow running; blue line = hopping; black line = at a reasonable tempo.

▷ Atomic game
The children run backwards and forwards all over the hall. Suddenly the trainer calls a number and the children get into groups of that number and hold each other's hands.

▷ Chasing race
2 teams are formed to run round the volleyball pitch, starting at any time on the centre line. Then the runners try and catch up with the other team.

Playful soccer training

▷ 3-mat soccer
Mats are set up as goals on 3 sides of the hall. Then 3 teams are formed and each team must defend a goal, whilst also being able to aim at the other 2 goals.

▷ 2/3 balls in play
We build mini-teams with 3 or at the most 4 players, playing with 2 or 3 balls. Who shoots the most goals in 5 minutes?

▷ Tournament
Small pitch tournament with 2-man teams.

H 3

Aim: To improve mobility and handling of the ball

Main points

All-round basic training

▶ Fire, water, earth

All the children run freely around in the sports hall and react as fast as they can to the following commands: fire = lie on your tummies on the ground; water = no contact with the floor, so climb up some apparatus; earth = hang on ropes, rings or ladders on the wall.

▶ Black and white

2 teams (black and white) lie down opposite each other at a distance of 2-3 metres on the centre line of the volleyball court. Then the trainer calls a colour. The colour called must catch the other. The teams can also sit back to back.

Playful soccer training

▶ Running and passing competition

Team A stands ready for running the gauntlet and passes the ball to each other, whilst team B sprints round the field. Then they change over.

▶ Team A again stands in running-the-gauntlet formation and passes the ball backwards and forwards. Team B runs one player behind another round the field once. How many passes does team A achieve in that time?

▶ Handball/ Soccer

2 teams play each other at soccer, where the ball may be played with the hand, but not catching the ball, only guiding it on.

H 4

Aim: To improve mobility and training ball sensitivity

Main points
All-round basic training
▶   Accordeon run
            Everyone runs from the front wall of the sports hall as far as
            the first marked line and back again, then as far as the 2nd,
            3rd and 4th line. Each time a line is reached, it must be
            touched with one's hand, elbow and bottom.
▶   Accordeon run with the ball
            The same exercise as above, but this time kicking a ball
            along.
▶   Balloon games

            We try to drive the balloon as fast as possible to the other
            side of the hall. We hold the balloon in the air with our head,
            feet, shoulder or thigh. Who can hold 2 or 3 balloons in the
            air at the same time?

Playful soccer training
▶   Guiding the ball
            We dribble the ball along in a pre-determined area backwards
            and forwards, making sure we don't touch another ball. A
            labyrinth of little flags is set up, through which the players
            dribble the ball. We try to kick the ball with one kick through
            the flag labyrinth, without touching a flag.
▶   Tournament
            To finish with, we play a tournament with 3-man teams. He
            who loses is out.

H 5

Aim: To train moving about and to improve ball sensitivity

Main points
All-round basic training

▶ Burning ball

2 teams are drawn up, throwing group A and catching group B. All the players spread out in the room. The throwing group throws the ball to each other and each completed throw gets a point. The catching group tries to catch the ball.

▶ Voelkerball with feet

The rules of "voelkerball" apply here, but the ball is only played with the feet. Any kind of touching means "caught". Anyone who has to jump in the air to avoid being hit by the ball is also "caught".

Playful soccer training

▶ Circuit

We set up 4 stages, for many players this means each stage twice:

1. 5 meters before the goal, the player throws the ball into the air and heads it into goal.
2. The player dribbles the ball down a slalom course of little flags and ends with a shot into goal.
3. The player tries to keep the ball in the air as long as possible with foot, hand, shoulder and thigh.
4. Tossing the ball, the player completes a sprinting run of between 10 and 15 metres.

▶ Soccer into handball goals

5-man teams play in a little tournament. Whoever loses 2 games is out.

H 6

Aim: Training mobility and ball sensitivity

Main points
All-round basic training

▷ Obstacle course
We build an obstacle course in a circle with the following stages:
Slalom-run around little cones or poles
Forward-rolls onto mats
Swinging on the ropes
Climbing over the wall of bars
Crawling through parts of boxes
Sprinting once round the hall
Throwing the ball into the basket
Shooting a goal from the 7-metre mark.

▷ This course can be made more difficult by building a ball into each exercise e.g. taking a medicine ball among whilst balancing.

▷ Children's imagination
2 children at a time work out together, which stage they will make up for the next circuit, which they then build up and present to their fellow players. Then a new circuit starts.

Playful soccer training

▷ Each player has a ball, which is sometimes tossed slowly or fast, or up into the air or onto the ground, changing the speed when the call is given. From this position we change into running and a different direction.

▷ We run round, tossing the ball and try to hit the ball away from our fellow players.

▷ Soccer and basketball
We each play 5 minutes of soccer into 2 goals, then 5 minutes of basketball and keep alternating.

H 7

Aim: To enjoy movement and goal-shooting

Main points
All-round basic training

▶   Hitting skittles
The volleyball pitch is used as our play area with both teams standing on the base line. Two long benches are set up on the centre line, on which cones or clubs are placed and then the players try to knock off the "skittles".

▶   Shooting skittles
The clubs can also be shot at if placed on the centre line without a bench.

▶   Catching game with intersection
To begin with, a catcher and someone to be caught are chosen. The other players help by thwarting the progress of the catcher and thereby reducing his speed.

Playful soccer training

▶   The living obstacle
Ten players position themselves as living obstacles on the field. They must always stop on one leg at the same place. Then another player tries to dribble through this "fellow players wood" ending with a shot into goal.

▶   Sections of boxes are put in front of the goal. After dribbling through the hall, there is a shot into goal, which must go through at least one box section.

▶   We play a small tournament with 3-man teams towards 2 box goals without goalkeeper.

H 8

Aim: To improve mobility and better handling of the ball

Main points
All-round basic training

▷ The prehistoric animal
5-8 children stand behind each other. Each child does the splits and grabs the left hand of the person behind by putting its right hand through its leg. Then the animal moves without the snake's falling apart.

▷ Hopping circle
The trainer stands in the middle of the sports hall swinging a rope. The children try and jump over the rope.

▷ Champion sprinter
From time to time from the top end of the hall we set 3 sprints going. We begin with a 5-metre sprint, followed by an 8-metre sprint, and then the third sprint goes as far as the centre line. A point is awarded each time the destination is reached. The winner is the one with the least points.

Playful soccer training

▷ Tossing the ball
We toss the ball on the spot. We toss the ball, do a forward roll and go on tossing it. We toss it through our legs whilst doing the splits. We toss it up and back down again with the right and left hand. We toss the ball whilst hopping, running backwards and during a sideways gallop.

▷ Dribbling the ball
We dribble the ball round obstacles. We dribble the ball and change direction.

▷ Game into 2 goals.

H 9

Aim: To train feeling for the ball and all-round mobility

Main points
All-round basic training

▷   Game with a frisbee
Working in pairs, we throw a frisbee to one another, and try and catch it. Whilst throwing, we stand inside a tyre, which we can only put one foot outside whilst throwing. Which team manages 10 throws without the frisbee touching the floor?

▷   Shadow running
5 players run after the person in front and copy all his movements. Each player has a ball. He must copy everything which the first player in the row does.

Playful soccer training

▷   4-goal game
At both ends and on the long sides of the hall there is a mat serving as a goal. Each team must now defend 2 goals, but can also at the same time attack 2 goals. Which team can score the most goals in 5 minutes?

▷   An unfair 4-goal game
This time team A must defend 3 goals and can only score successfully in one goal. But each goal scored is trebled compared with team B.

▷   A game of endurance
The players do 2-minute circuits of the hall kicking the ball and shooting it into each corner.

H 10

Aim: To get used to the ball and enjoy moving about

Main points

All-round basic training

▷   Carpet tiles

Carpet tiles are placed all over the hall for the children to jump and run over. We do final jumps over the tiles and then sit down on them from a running position when told to do so. We run round our tile and then push the tile a long way forwards whilst doing the splits.

▷   Goal shooter

Objects of various sizes are hung from the handball goal with string. These must first be hit by throwing the ball and then by kicking it.

Playful soccer training

▷   Running along the line with the ball

Each player runs along all the lines in the hall with a ball, first dribbling then tapping it up and down.

▷   Box soccer

At each end of the hall part of a box is placed about 3-4 meters from the wall. During a game with both teams, the goals may be shot at from all sides.

▷   Scuffle ball

2 mats placed at each end of the hall are the goals. The ball is now brought onto the mat by foot, hand or head.

H 11

Aim: To get used to the ball and improve one's feeling for movement

Main points
All-round basic training

▶ Play apparatus "beer mat"
Lots of beer mats are spread out across the floor. We run a slalom race round the mats, trying to jump over several mats. We balance a beer mat on our heads. We put a beer mat on our instep, flick it up and catch it.

▶ Keep the circle free
All beer mats are in the centre circle. One player throws them out into the hall. The other players collect them as fast as possible and put them back into the centre circle.

▶ Putting down pictures
All beer mats are spread out across the hall. Both A and B teams are awarded the picture side of a mat from time to time. Both teams run round and turn the mats onto their side. A count is made after the final whistle.

Playful soccer training

▶ Dribbling towards the goal
The players dribble through an alleyway of little flags and end with a shot into goal.

▶ Soccer towards long-bench goals
At each end of the hall is a long bench, tipped up so that the sitting side is where the goals will be shot. Then the teams play a tournament against each other. This can also be played with 2 balls.

H 12

Aim: To improve mobility and getting used to the ball

Main points
All-round basic training
▷   Voelkerball
    We play voelkerball with 2 soft balls. To make it more difficult to hit people, we build obstacles on the pitch e.g. boxes for people to hide behind.
▷   Movement stories
    The trainer sets up as many pieces of apparatus as possible in the hall, including balls. Then he tells a story with a wide variety of activities, which the players should use their imagination in carrying out, e.g. in the circus, Tarzan in the jungle, landing on strange stars, mountaineering.

Playful soccer training
▷   7-goal game:
    7-goal are set up in the hall using little cones. Play is always one to one. Goals can be scored at all 7 points, and if a player shoots a goal, then his partner gets the ball.
▷   Game with the wall
    The player shoots the ball flat onto the wall from a distance of 5 metres and then takes it again. The player shoots the ball halfway up the wall and takes it again. The player stands 2 metres away from the wall, throws the ball up, heads it onto the wall and catches it. The player tosses the ball at the wall and then stops it as it bounces back with his foot.

H 13

Aim: To train ball sensitivity and general mobility

Main points
All-round basic training

▷ Hunter ball

2 or 3 players as hunters try, whilst standing still, to hit their fellow players as they run round. He who is hit becomes hunter.

▷ Estimated running with the ball

All players run kicking the ball along through the hall and stop when they think that 2 minutes are up.

▷ 2 players pass the ball backwards and forwards to each other on the spot. When they think that 3 minutes are up, they stop.

Playful soccer training

▷ Guarding little cones

10 little cones are set up any way you like on the indoor pitch. 10 players now have the job of guarding these cones. 5 players, each with ball, try and hit a cone. Who can hit the most cones in 3 minutes? Then there's a change of task.

▷ 7-metre shooting

There's a goalkeeper in goal. All players shoot in turn. If the ball is stopped by the goalkeeper or shot past the goal the player has a turn in goal.

▷ Three-to-one

A goalkeeper stands in goal with a defence player in front of him. Three attacks try and shoot a goal. If the ball is touched by a defence, then he is swapped with the last person to touch the ball.

H 16

Aim: To improve agility and mobility

Main points
All-round basic training:
▷   Come with me – run away

4 long benches are placed in the form of a cross. 4 teams sit astride them. A runner runs round the whole square, taps a fellow-player on the back and calls "come with me!" or "run away". All the players on that bench carry out the command. Whoever reaches the bench last, runs round the square.

▷   Prize ball:

Team A runs along one side of the hall. Team B tries from the opposite side to hit the runners with a throw, then with a shot.

Playful soccer training
▷   Occupying tyres

Tyres lie spread out across the sports hall floor, not quite as many as the number of players. All the children dribble their ball around. At a shout from the trainer, each player must dribble his ball into a tyre and sit down.

▷   Sitting soccer

Goals are built from two mats at each end of the hall. The ball is now played sitting down.

▷   Spider soccer

All the players move around on their hands and feet and play follows according to recognized rules.

▷   Pot-luck shooting

Several tyres hang in both goals and then each player has 10 shots. Whoever manages to shoot through a tyre scores a point.

H 17

Aim: To improve skill and ball sensitivity

Main points
All-round basic training

▷   Play in stages

▷   1.   Soccer tennis: The pitch is marked off with small cones and 2 long benches are placed in the middle. Then 3-a-side play begins.

▷   2.   Box goals: 2 small box goals are built up across the hall. We play 3 against 3.

▷   3.   We play basketball onto a basket, again 3 against 3.

▷   Partner games
The partner is carried pig-a-back through the hall. The partner who is lying on the ground is jumped over. The partner who is lying on the ground like a bench is crawled under. The standing partner is hopped around on one leg.

Playful soccer training

▷   Shooting goals
A box is set up as a goal in each of the 4 corners of the hall and throughout the hall itself lots of apparatus is set up as obstacles. Each player dribbles around with his ball and should shoot the maximum number of goals.

▷   Running for a minute
We run around for about a minute and then sit down on a piece of apparatus. When exactly a minute has passed, the trainer blows his whistle. Who was the last to climb onto a box?

▷   Standing soccer
We play in 2 teams into goal, but whoever has the ball must not run but stand still.

Aim: To improve mobility and game culture

Main points

All-round basic training

▷ Circuit training in pairs

1. Throw the ball up and head it to one's partner, who catches it, throws it up etc.
2. The goalkeeper throws the ball to another player, who then heads it into goal with a forward dive.
3. Play one-to-one into a small goal.
4. 7-metre shot alternation between goalkeeper and goalshooter.
5. Each takes a turn at playing the ball onto the wall.

Playful soccer training

▷ Mimosa soccer

Whilst playing mimosa soccer, you're not allowed to touch another player. Whoever does this must sit on the ground for 30 seconds.

▷ Gangster soccer

There's a gangster hiding in each team. Without the other players knowing, he's picked by the trainer and must be discovered by his own team. The gangster is only allowed to play the ball back with his own team.

▷ Fool's soccer

The ball is played with all parts of the body. It can also be thrown or tossed with the hand, but it's forbidden to keep the ball in one's hand when running.

▷ An uneven tournament

There's a goalkeeper in every goal. Whilst team A has 4 players, team B has only 3. At the end the total number of goals is divided by the number of players.

H 19

Aim: To train ball sensitivity and improve mobility

Main points

All-round basic training

▷ Circuit training
1. The ball is juggled in the air after tapping it up once.
2. The ball is shot at the wall and caught again.
3. We dribble through a slalom alley several times.
4. We make various shots through a section of box.
5. We complete a throw at the wall and catch the ball again.
6. We throw the ball up, head it at the wall and catch it again.
7. We shoot through tyres hanging in the goal at varying heights.

Playful soccer training

▷ Goalkeeper training in pairs:
The goalkeeper stands at a distance of approximately 5 metres facing the hall wall. His partner shoots the ball at the wall and the goalkeeper catches it. After a while tasks change.

▷ Mat soccer:
Each wall of the hall has a mat serving as goal, and each mat is guarded by a goalkeeper. There are 2 balls on the go for both opposing teams, and a goal is scored when the ball touches a mat.

▷ Small tournament:
5-man teams are set up, who play in tournament formation.

H 20

Aim: To train ball sensitivity

Main points
All-round basic training

▷ Sprints with and without the ball
1. All players stand at the end of the hall. The trainer shoots a ball up and all the players set off to try and catch it.
2. All players shoot their ball from one end of the hall, run after it and try and stop it reaching the wall.
3. A player shoots the ball away from the end wall. All the players sprint after it and overtake the ball.

Playful soccer training

▷ Chasing race
4 teams stand in each of the 4 corners of the hall. When told to, they run off and try and catch up with the team which has already started. The same game is started, but each runner must dribble a ball along simultaneously with his hand. Then the same game is repeated with one's foot.

▷ Winning the ball
All the players but one have a ball to dribble round with. The player without a ball then manages to get a ball, after which the player left without ball, gets it off another player etc.

▷ A ball headed into goal scores double
In the closing tournament, every goal headed scores double in which heading the ball is especially practised.

In addition to the 60 training units for the sports ground and sports hall we should like next to give the children's trainer some exercises and games, with which we can strengthen his training programme at any time. Because, in principle, we are not just concerned with football, but also with improving the mobility and skill of the children, we have included fundamental patterns of movement, like running, jumping, throwing and climbing; but here as well, we want to do the action playfully.

12.1   The Ball Comes First

Simple movements with the ball come next, which "up-and-coming soccer players" must always master, if they want to learn how to manipulate the ball safely.

Dribbling with the ball

▷   We dribble at varying speeds.
▷   We dribble with the right and left foot.
▷   We dribble and stop as fast as possible when the trainer says so.
▷   We dribble, stop when told to, and sit on the ball.
▷   We dribble little and big circles first to the left and then to the right.
▷   Whilst dribbling we stop the ball with our foot, pull it back and carry on dribbling in another direction.

Kicks with the ball

▷   We kick the ball whilst stationary from the inside and then the outside.
▷   We kick the non-moving ball with our instep.
▷   We kick the ball with our strong and weak foot.
▷   We kick the ball after dribbling it.
▷   We kick the ball out of our hand.
▷   We kick the ball into a goal with goalkeeper.
▷   We kick the ball at a 1-metre-wide goal without goalkeeper.
▷   We kick the ball, as it is passed to us from the left or the right, into goal.

Juggling with the ball

▷ We juggle the ball as long as possible, first with some touching the floor and later with no touching the floor.

▷ We keep the ball in the air with our head.

▷ We juggle the ball on one thigh.

▷ We trap the ball between our feet and wriggle it upwards.

▷ We keep the ball in the air as long as possible with our head, thighs, feet and chest.

▷ We try and play the ball with our heel.

▷ All of these exercises can be played in pairs or groups of 3.

12.2 Co-ordination

▷ We run forwards, backwards and sideways with and without circling our arms.

▷ We do hopping and zigzag runs.

▷ We jump like a jumping jack.

▷ We jump with a rope forwards, backwards, with both legs, with one leg, with and without springing back in between.

▷ We sit down and stand up again without using our hands.

▷ While we are trotting round slowly, we do a jump and turn round completely on our own axis.

▷ We balance over an upside-down bench.

▷ We balance along a bench with a slight slope.

▷ We balance step by step along a little rope-walk, which is only one foot wide.

12.3 Pulling and Pushing Contests

▷ Wrestling match: 2 partners stand in a circle and each tries to force the other out, but not by using one's hands, which are kept close to one's body.

▷ Wrestling circle: Standing in a circle, 4 or 5 children hold each other's hands. Then each tries to make another go into the circle by pulling hard.

▷ Pulling a rope: The same number of children stand on either side of the rope and pull when told to. Which team pulls the other across the central point?

▷ Pushing match: 2 children stand opposite each other arms outstretched and holding each other. When told to, both start to push. Who can get his partner off the spot?

▷ Wobbly man: Both partners sit back to back with legs stretched out and arms linked. Both stand up and sit down again together.

▷ Two players grab hold of a medicine ball, one from the sides the other on top and underneath. When told to, each tries to pull the medicine ball out of the other's hand.

▷ Cock fight: With arms folded across their chest and hopping on one leg, the partners try to jostle and deceive each other. Whoever end up on both legs first, has lost the game.

12.4   Ball Magic

From time to time little competitions should be offered to the children. The winners and runners-up can then be given some sort of special recognition.

▷ *The ball magician*

Task 1: Who can juggle the ball most often with his foot in the air? Each has 3 attempts, of which the best counts.

Task 2: Who can keep the ball in the air longest with his foot? Here also 3 attempts are allowed.

Task 3: Who can dribble through a slalom course fastest? Only one attempt is permitted here. At all 3 stages, points are awarded and thus the best player is found.

▷ *Hall champion*

In the sports hall we can include the apparatus in our "canon" of tasks.

Task 1: Who is the fastest climber up the bars or the ropes?

Task 2: Who manages the most pull-ups on the horizontal bars?

Task 3: Who completes the fastest 10-metre run?

Task 4: Who can kick the medicine ball farthest?

Task 5: Who can balance the farthest on the upturned bench with built-in obstacles?

Task 6: Who can throw the ball farthest?

Task 7: Who can complete a run there and back kicking a ball and dribbling another ball with his hand?

Task 8: Who can move along a horizontal bar hanging by his hands?

Task 9: Who can get the most baskets from 5 attempts?

Task 10: Who can do forward and backward rolls alternately on 5 mats?

Skills contest

Task 1: We begin with alternating one-legged jumps over a rope lying on the floor – there with the right foot and back with the left.

Task 2: Keeping the football in the air with one's foot, turn round 3 times on one's own axis.

Task 3: We climb up a climbing pole.

Task 4: Shoot the ball into the air 3 times and stop it completely on the way down.

Task 5: We complete a series of squatting turns down an entire long bench.

Task 6: We lift the ball off the ground with our foot up onto our knee, from there onto our head, then back onto our knee and onto the ground. Each player has 3 attempts.

Task 7: Whilst juggling a balloon, we balance along a long bench, juggling with the right hand there and the left hand back.

Task 8: We punch a medicine ball with our right, our left and then both arms.

Task 9: The football must be shot with one kick through 3 one metre wide goals positioned behind each other.

Task 10: We run two rounds with the ball, one round tossing it and the other dribbling.

12.5   Games with and without the Ball

Board-handball

We draw up two 5-man teams. We play handball using the basketball boards as goals. If a basketball board is hit and then the ball falls to the ground, the throwing team gets a point. However, if the ball is caught by the defence team as it springs back from the board and before it reaches the ground, then the defence team gets a point.

Lion chase (light ball)

All the players form a bigger circle. 2 players stand in the middle behind, each other. The player behind gets hold of the front player's hips. The ball then circulates and specific shots should hit the back player on his back. The front player can ward off the ball with his hand.

Chase ball (light ball)
All the players form a circle in the middle of which is only one player. He must be hit, but if he catches a ball, he is released and replaced by the last thrower.

Rollball
Two benches turned onto their side (sports hall) or 2 small goals (outdoor pitch) are the aim of a football game. But this time the feet don't play and mustn't touch the ball. The ball is rolled along with the hand and must stay in contact with the ground.

Watchman's soccer
About 5 metres from the goal-line on each side a one square metre space is marked off, where the watchman sits. Then each team, when in possession of the ball, tries to play the ball to the watchman. The other team tries to prevent this and get the ball themselves. When a ball reaches a watchman, that team gets a point.

Hit ball
On either side of the field's outside line 5 players are standing. In exactly the middle of the field lie 5 balls. When given the signal, all start out together. One team wants to reach the other side, the other team runs to the balls in the middle and tries by throwing or shooting to knock off a player from the opposing team.

Striking
All the players form a circle, in which several balls are thrown around. 3 players are in the middle of the circle, who can hit the "circle players", when they have the ball. The ball must be passed amongst the circle players in such a way that it can be caught.

Ball over the cord-line
Two teams, divided by a cord, throw balls to each other, whereby the ball must be caught and not touch the ground. In order to make this catching a bit more difficult, various balls are in play e.g. a football, a handball, a volleyball, a basketball, a medicine ball.

Soccer with the rugby ball
2 teams play according to soccer rules. As the ball makes unusual movements, this game contains a lot of surprises.

Partner-burning ball

2 teams of equal numbers are drawn up. The throwing side stands on the field base line, the field where the catching side has taken up position. There are little flags at the 4 corners of the field, which serve as running markers. In an exactly pre-determined order, the first pair throws a ball far out onto the field, then they run off hand in hand in order to reach a running marker or to complete a full round. The catching side must get the ball as fast as possible and play the ball to the catcher at the burning marker (mat). If the runners at this point are between 2 running markers, they're out. If a whole round is managed on one throw, the throwing side gets 2 points, if the round is completed in stages, then there's 1 point; As an alternative, footballers can also shoot the ball of course i.e. the catching side must kick the ball along to the burning marker.

Rounds soccer

At each corner of the field 4 or 5 players are sitting, each with a ball. When told to, they all dribble a round of the whole field. Which team is sitting complete back in its corner first?

Taxi soccer

4 areas (4 square metres in size) are marked out as taxis on a defined playing field. All the players dribble around with the ball. Then the trainer calls a number. So many players can now get into each taxi, but whoever doesn't get a seat, is awarded a minus point.

Joker soccer

Two equally strong teams try on a pre-marked field (penalty area) to pass the ball to each other within their ranks. A joker plays in each team, whom the other team doesn't know. Each pass, which reaches the joker, gets the team a point.

Soccer versus handball

2 teams of equal numbers play into 2 goals. In the first half, team A plays with their feet and team B with their hands. The handball players may only receive the ball, if it doesn't touch the ground, so only from high balls. In the second half roles are reversed. Which team is the more successful?

Twin soccer

2 teams play into little goals, but two children, who have linked themselves together, must play together and not let go of each other.

All join in

We play with two 4-man teams against each other, but a goal can only be scored, if all players in one team have touched the ball during an attack. If a player from the partner team gets the ball in the meantime, the attack starts all over again.

Goalkeeper, come on!

Of course our teams play fair, but this time we've a new rule. If a player commits a foul, which is recognised by the trainer and causes him to blow the whistle, then he has to enter goal as goalkeeper. He can only be released by being a good goalkeeper. If he succeeds in stopping three goals from the opposing team, he can become a field player again and the original goalkeeper resumes his position.

Penalty soccer

Fair play is the aim of all teams, so this time fouls will be severely penalized. For every foul, there's a penalty, no matter where it has happened. The fouled player sees to it himself. He runs unimpeded but fast from the centre line to the opposing goal and he then has one shot. If the ball goes straight into goal, the hit counts. As soon as the goalkeeper touches the ball, the player has lost and play resumes from a kick-off.

12.6   Playing on Gym Apparatus

During training time in the sports hall, apparatus can also be used, but ensuring that their usage is playful. Whenever using apparatus, the trainer should be aware of the safety measures available by using mats and helpful positions.

The apparatus garden

All sports hall apparatus is built into an apparatus garden, in which the players can do gymnastics, balance, climb, hang along bars, swing and much more besides.

One player shows how to climb through the garden and the others copy.

We form pairs. One player has the job of guiding a blind person (eyes blindfolded) through the garden.

Whilst playing in the apparatus garden we keep a balloon in the air, without the players touching the ground.

▶ All the players move about in the apparatus garden until a call from the trainer indicates certain tasks to be fulfilled e.g. hanging from, standing on, sitting on or lying on a piece of apparatus.

Each set of parallel bars has two bars

▶ We hang onto the bars like a lazybones and don't move.
▶ A real lazybones can even let an arm or a leg hang down.
▶ A lazybones climbs through the parallel bars.
▶ We wriggle our legs in a resting position.
▶ Who can hang along the bars?
▶ Who can creep over the bars on all fours?

Horizontal bar, but not too high

▶ We hang and swing on the horizontal bar.
▶ We hang on the horizontal bar, with a ball pinched tight between our legs, swing and jostle the ball against the wall or into a box.
▶ One player, as goalkeeper, hangs on the horizontal bar and tries to ward off balls thrown at him with his feet. The hanging player must be changed over frequently.

Now it's time to climb

▶ We climb up the ropes.
▶ Who can climb up a rope without using his feet?
▶ We climb up a rope, change over onto a neighbouring rope at the top and let ourselves down to the ground again.
▶ We climb round the whole horse once like Indians.
▶ We climb up and down the horizontal bars.
▶ We climb round other players who are hanging on the bars.

Keeping one's balance nicely

A long bench is turned over and used as balancing apparatus:

▶ We balance with our feet at an angle forwards and backwards.
▶ We balance setting one foot in front of the other.
▶ We walk behind each other in pairs and the person behind holds the person in front round his hips.
▶ We walk back to back along the bench.
▶ We balance in pairs along the bench linking arms together at our side.

▶ Whilst balancing, we climb through a ring, held out by a fellow player.

▶ We climb over objects (medicine ball, bar, club) which are lying on the bench.

▶ We roll a medicine ball in front of us along the bench.

▶ Two children start, one at each end of the bench, and try to find a way of passing each other.

Mats – nice and comfortable

Lots of mats are laid out, including a soft-bottomed mat if available.

▶ We drop onto the soft-bottomed mat as dramatically as possible.

▶ One player drops into a special pose and his fellow players guess, what he's trying to be. Who has the most original idea?

▶ We run round the mats and fall onto another mat when told to.

▶ We hop from mat to mat.

▶ We hop like a frog from mat to mat.

▶ We put the mats so close together that they can be jumped over. Then all the players jump across the mat ditches.

▶ We run over all the mats doing a forwards or backwards roll on each one.

▶ We try to run across all the mats only touching them once.

12.7   Running, Jumping, Throwing

3 basic principles, which a good soccer player should master. So, we should like to incorporate a few aspects of track-and-field athletics, as we're concerned with the training of basic forms of movement.

Running fast and keeping going

▶ We run in figures e.g. a circle, a square, a figure-of-eight, a question mark, a date of birth, a forename in capital letters etc.

▶ On the field or in the sports hall stages are set up using the apparatus or balls. All stages are then run off in any order one chooses.

▶ We run without a watch. Each person should run for 3 minutes. If he thinks his time is up, he sits down. Who has a good sense of time?

▷ A sprinters triple contest is started with starts over 5 metres, 10 metres and 15 metres.

▷ We run 3 rounds of the pitch at warming-up speed, but one goal-line must be run along fast on each round.

▷ For a chasing race, all players stand at the start. One player suddenly starts with no signal. His fellow players must have overtaken him within 30 metres.

Long and high jumps

▷ We begin with long jump from a position of standing still and jumping off both legs.

▷ Zone-long jump: We organize 5 zones at a distance of 30-50 cm. The first zone starts 1 metre behind the jumping off zone. Each player now chooses only 2 zones, which he wants to reach, come what may, and with only 3 attempts allowed.

▷ Triple jump on one leg: from a stepping position we complete 3 jumps with our stronger leg.

▷ High jump: at a measuring batten we are allowed 3 high jump attempts. The best jump is recorded and then calculated: height of jump minus body length.

▷ We hop on our right or left leg. When the trainer says so, we do a one-legged jump as high as possible.

Soccer players need throwing power

▷ We throw a medicine ball to each other in pairs, first throwing it off with both arms on one's chest, then with the right arm, left arm and over one's head.

▷ We set up 50-metre zones just inside the kicking-off line. Then follows a medicine ball triple contest. Each player has a throw with the right arm, the left arm and both arms.

▷ Rubber rings should be thrown as far as possible.

▷ Rubber rings should be thrown into tyres or other specific areas of the field.

▷ Who can, with one throw of the football, get it farthest after 3 attempts; first with stationary throws then with a run up to it?

▷ Driving with a rounders ball: Two players keep on throwing a rounders ball to each other. By throwing as far as possible – having started on the centre line – each tries to "throw" the other one off the field.

13. EXPERIENCING COMMUNITY SPIRIT IN A CLUB

Even the young kickers know and experience that soccer is a team game. So the foundation is already laid here through sport for experiencing a team as a community. In this way team spirit grows and can be transferred to other non-sporting activities. These are especially important today, because lots of children, particularly only-children, seek and need friends to play with, in order to learn how to socialize properly with their own age-group. It's not only playing together which achieves this, but also being together in the rest of their free time.

That's why a supervisor of children's teams needs special qualifications to become a trainer. However, he also needs teaching ability, especially in the field of communication. For many children, soccer is more then just sport; they want to play together, travel, go hiking, have parties, have fun, experience things and much more besides. Through all this, more or less intensive contact to the supervisor develops slowly, but also to the other players, which can be summed up as a kind of "We-feeling". Naturally, every child wants to be a part of that.

Today, the non-sporting structuring of children's leisure time – referring continually to both boys and girls – is at least as important for the development of most children as everything offered to them in training and playing. Therefore, every children's supervisor must understand the main emphasis in this area. Moreover, he has here the opportunity of gaining fully-responsible and involved parents for his team work, and all this in the knowledge that education work, because that is what this activity must be called, can yield totally successful results for all those involved, when liaising with the parents. At this point, one shouldn't forget the tip that other people can also be gainfully employed in this process e.g. schoolteachers, who are interested in sport, well-known players from the first team, kinder-garten helpers and teachers, a particularly fit grandpa as well as any other sportenthusiast friends and relations.

13.1   Our Team Celebrates

There are innumerable reasons for children to have a party. With a bit of imagination, one can always find and "discover" ways of relaxing

normal daily and routine with a party. Firstly, there are all the usual annual celebrations with traditional background, which determine the days for a celebration. But there are also more variable occasions, extending into spontaneous activities and improvised celebrations.

One shouldn't forget that children like to help get ready for a party, because for them enjoying the preparations is sometimes more important and eventful than the party itself. This tip already indicates that children are full of inspiration in this area and will willingly participate if they are motivated to do so. Another important tip: Children's parties should be full of variety, activity and movement, which means that they are put together differently than those of adults and young people.

Celebrations during the year

The calendar year has specific dates, when children want a party for their team.

BIRTHDAY

Birthdays are special events in a child's life which it looks forward to, so what could be more important than letting one's fellow players share this happiness, which can be done in a variety of ways.

> The birthday child can play his favourite training game with everybody.

> The birthday child invites his team to a birthday party when the training session is over (Corner of the playing field, gym, youth centre, garden, woods etc.). Entertaining children's games with little prizes are organized.

> The birthday child invites both teams to cocoa, tea and cake or to a glass of lemonade after play has finished. Then various entertaining games follow, where both teams mixed up about in a lively way.

> The birthday child invites everyone after training to a paper-chase. Once the goal has been discovered, all wait for a surprise.

> The birthday child entertains his fellow players with a play from the puppet theatre.

CHRISTMAS CELEBRATION

If it has been decided to celebrate Christmas with the team or a group of children, then parents and other relations (brothers and sisters, grandparents) should be invited. The children should also be in no doubt that they are the organisers.

▶ There must be music at a Christmas party. Community Christmas carols are sung (text provided), which can have an instrumental accompaniment. There may well be children in the group, who play an instrument themselves and can perform something.

▶ A Christmas party needs a Christmas story. This can be enacted by the children in various roles or read out. Sometimes the children's imagination is so good that they can invent their own Christmas story.

▶ A vital ingredient of Christmas parties is the reading of Christmas poems, and for those who have difficulty in reciting a poem by heart they can certainly read out loud.

▶ Presents are quite indispensable at a Children's Christmas party. But these shouldn't just have been bought in a shop, but rather have a personal touch and give pleasure to the recipient. Everyone participating brings a small personal present and puts it in the big present sack at the beginning of the party. He adds a label with a few friendly words and "signs" it with his forename. Father Christmas ultimately distributes presents to everyone.

▶ Perhaps the children could go without a present voluntarily. Instead, trainers, supervisors and coaches get a home-made present from the children as a reward for their work: What about writing the trainer a nice poem and everyone signing it?

Special occasion parties

Parties or celebrations, whether planned or spontaneous are fixed points for dividing up everyday life and giving their souls a breath of air. There is a pleasing number of such occasions.

▶ The team has a sporting victory to celebrate like the first win of the season, the first away win, champions of the league, winning a tournament.

▶ The team receives an invitation from a supervisor, coach, some parents or a patron.

▶ A new player joins the team, or a new trainer or children's supervisor. Both welcoming a new person in, as well as saying goodbye are celebrated.

▷ The trainer invites everyone to a sports or teaching film "soccer". One member of the team shows pictures or a film of an interesting journey.

▷ The whole team visits an international game or national league game in their area.

▷ A kicking tournament, table-tennis or badminton tournament is organized.

▷ In the Winter, the whole team visits the ice stadium or goes to a Christmas pantomime.

▷ In the Summer, the parents organize a barbecue in one of their gardens or at a barbecue area in the woods.

▷ In the holidays, a night hike, woodland rallye or animal watch is organized.

This list of suggestions can be extended any way one likes, but as far as the planning by those in charge is concerned, local possibilities must be discovered and made note of. Sporting, social and cultural aspects should all be considered.

13.2 Our Team on Tour

Travel educates, so people say, but also brings people closer together. So soccer teams go off on day-trips or trips lasting several days, in order to strengthen a sense of community within the team, as it's shared experiences which really join people together.

Various aspects should be borne in mind when planning and undertaking such trips:

▷ The chosen destination should suit the children's stage of development and take account of their strong urge to move about. That means that longer journeys with a lot of sitting down are to be avoided. What appeals to children? Here are a few guidelines: animal parks, adventure playgrounds, boat trips, farms, pony rides, covered-wagon rides, trip to an airport, zoo, ice stadium etc.

▷ An invitation is sent out to parents giving a clear plan of the outing, meeting place and costs, where the parents must give their written consent on a detachable strip of paper. One should also ask about any special requirements for the children (e.g. liable to be travel-sick etc.)

▷ There should be a few serious words with the children prior to departure concerning their behaviour (cleanliness, punctuality, following instructions etc.). Keeping to the rules ensures corporate safety and avoids any negative atmosphere.

▷ In principle only the front door is opened during a bus journey, where a responsible adult always sits, so that all getting in and out can be checked. Particular care should be taken when the bus comes in ready for boarding.

▷ All instructions concerning organization are given to the children in the bus. A bus journey can also be made more interesting through things like: the children tell each other stories, something is read out, an amusing children's video etc.

▷ Whenever the children are free to move about in a defined area, the time and place to meet again must be made clear, and the time they have to themselves should be kept short. Also, the children should move around the area in small groups and always be aware, where one of their supervisors is.

▷ Everyone can look forward to an enjoyable outing, if they all try and keep to the agreed regulations.

13.3 Holiday arrangements

More and more clubs are starting to offer some special holiday experience for children. Children are attracted towards the idea of enjoying one or two weeks' holiday amongst others of their own age. But here also, responsible planners should bear a few principles in mind.

▷ It is not a case of the further one goes the better! Rather one should concentrate on making the holiday time as imaginative as possible.

▷ Therefore it's important when choosing the accommodation (comp-site, youth centre, a holiday park etc.), to look for the sort of space where the team can really come together. The conditions are especially favourable if the group can be for themselves.

▷ The cost of such an undertaking should be as low as possible. This can be achieved by planning ways of getting there, parental transport (they fetch and carry the children) and partly through self-catering. If there are any socially-deprived children, those in charge should find tactful way of including them, so that nobody has to stay at home for financial reasons.

▷ The dates should be fixed as early as possible and parents and children notified. Moreover, someone should be made responsible for answering any queries that may arise.

▷ When choosing accommodation, one should make sure that there are things to do in bad weather, i.e. it's important that the group has its own common room, is near a sports ground, a sportshall and swimming pool. The local traffic situation around the proposed accommodation should not be overlooked, so that the children's safety is guaranteed.

▷ Included in the information given out to parents should be the indication that any gross infringement of the agreed rules means the return of the child to its parents.

▷ As far as the planned structure of an activity holiday is concerned, those in charge must make double plans i.e. for normal and bad weather. Also the children should bring their favourite party games with them, which can be used in the evening or when it rains.

▷ As far as sport is concerned – which must also be planned for at holiday time – new games are learnt and special kinds of tournaments organized.

▷ If the club can't find enough supervisors in its ranks, then parents or older players can sometimes be persuaded to take on such a task.

Bibliography

Albeck, Th./Zöller, H.: Kindgerechtes Fußballtraining, Handbuch für Jugendtrainer und Sportlehrer/innen, WFV-Schriftenreihe, Bd. 27.

Bauer, G: Über die Bedeutung „sensibler Phasen" für das Kinder- und Jugendtraining, in: Leistungssport 4/87, S. 4-10.

Baur, J.: Jugendfußball heute, in: Fußballtraining 8/9/87, S. 9-14.

Bischops, K./Gerards, H-W.: Handbuch für Kinder- und Jugendfußball, Aachen, 2. Aufl., 1994.

Bischops, K./Gerards, H-W.: Tips für Spiele mit dem Fußball, Aachen 1989.

Bomers, H.: Fußball-Kartothek 5, Münster 1993.

Bremer, D.: Jugendfußball heute, in: Fußballtraining 8/9/88, S. 31-36.

Brüggemann, D.: Kinder- und Jugendtraining, Fußball-Handbuch 2, Schorndorf 1989.

Deutscher Fußball-Bund (Hg.): Fußball-Lehrplan 2: Kinder- und Jugendtraining, Grundlagen, München 1985.

Deutscher Fußball-Bund (Hg.): Fußball-Lehrplan 3: Kinder- und Jugendtraining, Aufbau und Leistung, München 1987.

Hahn, E.: Kindertraining, Probleme, Trainingstheorie, Praxis und Sportwissen, München/Wien/Zürich 1982.

Hahn, E.: Kindertraining. München, 1982

Hamsen, G./Daniel, J.: Fußballtraining, Reinbek 1990.

Liessen, H./Hollmann, W.: Die Ausdauerfähigkeit bei verschiedenen Sportarten unter besonderer Berücksichtigung des Metabolismus. In: Beiheft zu Leistungssport 9/1977, S. 63-79

Martin, D.: Nachwuchstraining in der Diskussion, in: Leistungssport 5/87, S. 16.

Martin, D.: Training im Kindes- und Jugendalter, Studienbrief der Trainerakademie des DSB, Bd. 23, Schorndorf 1988.

Nickel, H.: Entwicklungspsychologie des Kindes- und Jugendalters, Bd. 2.

Pfeifer, W./Maier, W.: Fußball-Praxis, Jugendtraining II, 4. Teil: Technik, Taktik, Kondition, WFV-Schriftenreihe, Nr. 20.

Rowland, T. W.: Exercise and children's health. Champaign, IL: 1990

Seefeldt, V.: The future of youth sports in America. In: F. L. Smoll & R. E. Smith (Eds.), Children in sport: A biopsychosocial perspective (pp. 423 – 435). Indianapolis, 1996

Schmidt, W.: Kindheit, Jugend und Fußballzugang im Wandel, in: BDFL-Journal 8/94, S. 55-64.

Wittmann, F./Maier, W./Pfeifer, W.: Fußball-Praxis, Jugendtraining I, 3. Teil: Leistungsbestimmende Grundlagen, Mannschaftsführung, WFV-Schriftenreihe, Bd. 15.

Zeitschriften

Leistungssport: Zeitschrift für die Fortbildung von Trainern, Übungsleitern und Sportlehrern, Herausgeber: DSB, Münster.

Der Fußballtrainer: Fachzeitschrift für alle Trainings- und Wettkampffragen, Reutlingen.

Fußballtraining: Zeitschrift für Trainer, Sportlehrer und Schiedsrichter, Herausgeber: Bisanz, G., Münster.